SLAVE

This book is a work of non-fiction based on the life, experiences and recollections of Anna, the author. In some cases names of people/places/dates/sequences of the detail of events have been changed.

SLAVE

ANNA

with Jason Johnson

EBURY
PRESS

12

Ebury Press, an imprint of Ebury Publishing
20 Vauxhall Bridge Road
London SW1V 2SA

Ebury Press is part of the Penguin Random House group of companies whose
addresses can be found at global.penguinrandomhouse.com

Penguin
Random House
UK

First published by Ebury Press in 2018

www.penguin.co.uk

A CIP catalogue record for this book is available from the British Library

ISBN 9781785038983

Typeset in 11.25/16 pt Garamond MT Pro
by Integra Software Services Pvt. Ltd, Pondicherry

Printed and bound in Great Britain by Clays Ltd, Elcograf S.p.A.

Chapter One

They took me because I would not be missed.

It is not a simple thing to steal someone and not put them back. Some people will miss the person; they will wonder where they went. They might call the police, go to their house, go looking through the things they left behind.

They might put up posters or go on television to say, 'Where has this person gone? Can someone help me find this person? This person has disappeared into thin air.'

But with me, none of that happened. To know that I was alone, without people who would fight to find me, was all they needed to know. I was a young female from Romania in among people who were coming and going all the time in a big, foreign city and, as is the way of these things, I was just a face in the crowd. So they took me. It was like no crime had been committed. There was only thin air left behind and no one really noticed. And, you know, I still think sometimes, 'How clever of them.'

From that day they called me 'the blind one'. They would always say 'Where is the blind one?' or 'How many has the blind one done?' or 'The blind one has been making trouble again.'

That was my name maybe because it was the first weakness they discovered when they took me. My glasses came off as they pulled me into the car.

The first thing I said to them was, 'Give me back my glasses.'

And in those moments they looked at my glasses, turned them over and could see that they were strong, that these were not just for reading, that they were glasses for living, needed by someone who does not see well.

So they laughed and called me 'blind' and then 'the blind one' and put my glasses somewhere. I don't know where they went, but it is maybe strange to think they kept them very safe. They made sure they were not broken so that when the time was right, when I was the thing that was broken, they could give them back to me again.

And, after four months, when they said to themselves, 'She is ours now, she has given up, she is no danger to us now,' they gave me back my glasses.

For four months I lived like someone used to live, before glasses were invented, with poor eyesight, with sore eyes and many headaches and without really being able to see anything or anyone very well. It was a new world for me, a place where I did not fit, which was often out of focus.

And then they said, 'Here you are, you can wear these now. Do not ever say that we don't give you anything.'

Chapter Two

It was 11 March 2011. It was Friday.

The morning was sunny and mild – not warm, not cold. I remember thinking how nice it was when I closed the door at 7.30am.

The street in north London I had been living on is called Westbury Avenue. It is a long street with lots of terraced houses and some trees and, at one end, some shops, a pub, some places to eat. It's a pleasant area, people coming and going and not bothering each other and sometimes smiling as they walk past you.

The Tube stations closest to me were Wood Green and Turnpike Lane, but you should not think that I used either of them very much. Most of the time when I travelled in London I would take the bus, sitting on the top floor and listening to my music and looking out.

The Tube I think is a good place to look at people and quickly walk through tiled tunnels and stand looking at posters in stations where the only wind is from the trains, if that's what you want to do. But if you want to look at buildings or roads, if you like to look at the city itself, you will not see it down there. You don't know where you are in the Tube; you have no real understanding of where you are going. The truth is I felt better being on buses than on Tube trains, so I took the bus.

I got on board near Turnpike Lane station at 7.45am to be at my work in Finchley for 8am or a little bit after. The cosmetic surgeons who owned the house didn't mind if I was a little late or early. I had come to clean the house for two hours and I would be there for two hours, so if I arrived at 8.10am their daughter would still be nice and say 'Good morning' and ask how I was. I would tell her I was 'Fine, thanks' and say 'Hello' to their dogs and we would both go about our business.

So I did some ironing and cleaning the kitchen and the bathrooms and after two hours I left.

I walked for about ten minutes to the second place, where a man lived on his own. Sometimes he was there, sometimes he wasn't, but I had a key to his house, like I had a key to nearly all of the houses I cleaned.

I didn't know this man very well but he was getting older and I knew he really did need someone to help him keep things clean. The kitchen wasn't good and I don't think he knew how to operate his dishwasher. He would put filthy dishes in it, the food not even scraped from the plates, and close the door and forget about it.

I was there for nearly two hours, cleaning the kitchen, cleaning out and starting the dishwasher, cleaning the bathrooms and washing some clothes. The toilet in his house was – well, you don't need to know.

It was nearly 1pm when I had finished the two jobs and I was taking my lunch break. I had another job starting in the afternoon in Wood Green and that would be for two hours again, because that was the amount of time many people thought was enough.

On those days, when I had one hour or more between jobs, I would go back to Westbury Avenue to eat and watch television. My breakfast on that day had been only a croissant and Coke, as it usually was, and I was hungry. Going home to relax and eat and watch television, without having to pay anything or see anyone while I was dressed in my work clothes, was a good idea.

I took the bus to Wood Green and remember thinking it might rain later in the day, that the London sky had become a little bit darker. I got off to walk along the road towards my house. If you want to picture me, you should know I had my earphones in and my glasses on and I was wearing my grey winter coat, furry at the neck.

I was wearing a dark T-shirt and some trousers and flat shoes I used for work, which were not too fashionable.

I was in a little world of my own just going along, not happy, not sad, with my head tipped down towards the pavement because I am not a girl who always has my head up.

I was coming close to my house, maybe three doors or four doors away, when I walked past a dark-red car that had pulled up, facing me, along the side of the street. There were people in it – two people in the front, a man and a woman. They were looking straight ahead, not talking.

Why would I care about this? I didn't. But I remember looking at the car and those people and thinking, 'Why are they just sitting still like that, like dummies?' I don't remember if the engine was running.

I walked some more steps and was maybe two houses before my own house. I heard no car door, no one saying anything. All

5

I could hear was music, just Beyoncé singing into my ears. Then I felt a hand grab tight on the back of my neck. An arm came to the front of my face and it covered my mouth. I fell backwards – was tugged backwards – and then more hands were pulling at my shoulders, dragging me.

I don't remember thinking about trying to fight or bite but all my limbs were moving, my arms and feet trying to hit at someone I couldn't see. I can only tell you that I was pulled hard and fast, deep into the car, hitting my hands on everything as I went in. I was not strong enough or lucky enough to damage anyone.

Someone closed the door from the outside and got into the front of the car. I screamed at her, at everything, as she got back into her passenger seat with my glasses in her hand. I shouted some kind of word, maybe in English, maybe German, Romanian. It was the first sensible noise I had been able to make but I don't know what it was.

The man in the back pushed me off him and said, 'Sshhh.'

I pulled myself up to the door at my side. I knew he had my bag and I could see him looking inside, so I started to hit him. He tucked his head down and I slapped and scratched hard at his face and his head. The woman started slapping me on the back of the head and the side of my face. She punched into the side of my head and the man pushed me back. She hit me more, hard, and I did not hit her. I did not know if I was bleeding.

The music had stopped. I could see the wires from my earphones hanging down against my coat, but not clearly. The noise in my ears was loud from the hitting, a kind of ringing sound, like a kind of siren. I lifted my face up to look in front of me and I could see the woman, sitting up between the two seats, ready to hit me again. She seemed lean but strong, very determined. And she was very angry, as if I had done something wrong to her.

I knew she was Romanian. I had seen her before, I knew her face and I already wanted never to see it again. I had seen the man beside me too; his face was known to me from somewhere. I wasn't sure about the driver. I knew for sure that they were all Romanian, but the next thing I said was in English. I wiped at my nose and said, 'Will you give me back my glasses?'

And she shook her head and looked down at the glasses in her hand. She was turning them over as if examining them.

'She is blind,' she said, in Romanian, looking back up at me.

The man in the front said, in Romanian, 'Ah, blind,' as if it meant something, but he was not looking at me when he spoke. He was looking into the side mirror of the car, already turning onto the road and driving away.

I had not heard the car start. It was maybe already running before they took me. I could not work out what was going on but I knew of course it was all bad.

The man beside me passed the bag into the front of the car and the woman started looking inside. My hand went, as if by itself, to take it back, to reach over and grab it, and the man at my side hit me for the first time. He punched me, with his fist, on my jaw. I felt my teeth hit into each other and it made me stop moving. His name is Carol, a boy's name in eastern Europe, a girl's name in the west.

I sat there as she looked in the bag, my face and head hurting. I felt as if someone had been pulling my hair but I couldn't remember anyone pulling my hair.

So now maybe I was being robbed? This was the first sense I was making of what was happening. And I considered then that I didn't care if I was being robbed, as long as they stopped the car and kicked me out.

I looked down at the wires hanging over my coat and pulled at them, at the earphones, as if to get them off me. Carol was watching, watching me and my clothes, and reached over and into my pocket, knowing my phone was there, like a practised thief. He handed it into the front.

He didn't know I had another one, one I used only for work, in another pocket. Straight away I thought, 'Be careful with this one. Always think twice and keep this other phone.'

And it was clear now that I would be hit again at any second. It was clear that I was trapped in a car with three people. It was clear that they didn't care that I had seen all their faces. That is not how you would rob someone.

Now my breathing was deep, not that fast but the breaths were deep as if my body was trying to make itself calm, making itself ready.

I told myself I had not yet tried to get out of the door, that I had not yet pulled the handle right beside me. It had been seconds, maybe a minute, but I had still not done the most sensible thing of them all and tried to open the door. I told myself we were moving on a road but that when we slowed or stopped I could finally be brave enough to grab the handle, get out and run for my life. This is what people do when they are trapped in cars, when they want to get away. I told myself that was how I would get away.

But do those people trapped in cars think what I was thinking? Do they start to count? You see, it would take me two or three seconds to open the door but the man was less than a second from reaching me. The woman was as close to me as he was.

And I told myself, 'What if there is a child-lock?' I asked myself, 'What will happen if I pull this and the door doesn't open?'

I was not feeling brave. My head was saying, 'Don't let yourself get hit again,' and 'Just ask them what it is you can do for them.' It said, 'If you try to pull this handle on this door you will be hit and hit and hit, it would be an obvious mistake to make.' I did not think I could get away from this car but there was still something telling me I had to try.

So I waited until the moment was right.

And it came to me, the woman's name. She was Crina and she was Carol's girlfriend. Crina and Carol. It all came to me in an instant after somehow not realising it at all at first. They even lived in the same house that I lived in. They shared a room upstairs. They were one of the couples in the house, a big house owned by a Romanian landlord who lived there too. I didn't know this couple personally, only to see their faces, to hear their low voices as they walked past my door, but now, suddenly, I knew them.

This stranger, Crina, worked in a strip club. And now she was looking at other people's keys in my bag, now she was going through my wallet checking how much was in there. She was looking at everything I had, at anything that might be of use to her or might interest her.

I was thinking, 'Who are you to do this to me?'

And then she started with my phone, looking at the names of the people I had been calling, at the connections I had made on Facebook, mostly friends from back in Romania.

She turned to me, looking at me looking at her and hating her already, and I didn't know if I should look away.

In Romanian, she said, 'I have to tell you Anna that if you want your mother to die then you can scream. Do you understand?'

Carol said, 'So do you want to scream now? Go ahead and scream now. And we promise your mother in Sibiu will die, okay?'

Crina said, 'She is called Anna too, isn't she?'

I didn't answer. I had been hit again by another shockwave, by another kind of a punch from this woman's words.

Carol said, 'Isn't she?'

And I said, 'Da.'

It means 'Yes'.

Because my mother is Anna too.

Crina nodded and went back to looking at what she was doing again, looking at the girls I knew on Facebook, looking at parts of my life she had no business to see.

The car was then on a bigger road and moving faster. I do not remember if it had stopped or really slowed down at all. But I remember that it started to move faster and that the man in the back gave everyone a cigarette. He didn't offer me one and it's strange because I don't know if I would have taken it. I think maybe I would have done so.

I wanted to look out of the windows, to really see the roads, but it felt like I might be in trouble if I did, if I tried to see the names of the places we were passing. I think it is a normal reaction when a person is scared, to want to sit still, to not draw attention to yourself.

It was when I was looking ahead, controlled and still, that I saw a high-up sign telling me what road we were going along. It said 'Luton Airport'.

I think maybe it was then, just about that moment, that I did the clearest thinking since I had been pulled into the car. The craziness of it all was not crazy to these people. They had to have some reason. And I think it was after those first few minutes that I began to understand what they wanted me for.

This was what I had heard about, this was to do with sex, with prostitution. They were going to take me somewhere, tell me some things that terrified me, tell me to make money for them. This is the true horror story that people in Romania have been hearing for years, the story that silly girls who leave are being tricked and trapped and forced into selling themselves for someone else's pocket.

And, you know, I had no doubt in my mind that, if I was right, I would not be a victim of that. I would not be a prostitute. This is an insane thing to even think. This would not be me.

I thought, 'How bad can something like this get?'

I considered how I must, without any doubt, wait until the right moment to run away from this, to use my phone, to help myself and get help. I thought it just cannot be impossible for me to escape from these three people and this car.

And I tell you this – I had not one clue in the world, not one single idea.

They knew much more than I thought. You see, they had already found out I carried my passport with me because it had been stolen from my room before. They knew it would be with me, probably in my bag, as I walked down the street alone from work. They knew the simple truth that a passport and a ticket are the only two things it takes to get someone out of one country and into another.

So, as I told you, I had not one clue. I never did use the handle on the car door. I never did find the perfect moment I had been waiting for, the moment to escape and run free. I think I just entertained myself with childish thoughts of escape that day because I did not want to make room for other thoughts.

Chapter Three

I have one piece of good advice and, if you want to know it, it is this – always leave a trail.

If you are a criminal or a cheat or an animal that is hunted by other animals, it's bad advice. But if you are an ordinary person with nothing to hide, you should think about it.

It is never a mistake to be able to retrace your steps or to have the ability to show others where you have been. If you leave a trail, people can know your journey. If you can keep evidence with you of where you have been, then you can tell people the story of where you went, maybe of who you are.

A trail means there is always a chance that you will be able if necessary to show people the truth, that you will always be able to help yourself, or be found, if you are lost. It means you are organised and thinking and that you know a map is more valuable than a mystery. People make up their own minds about other people all the time, instantly, before they know anything. If you have your story, if they can know your story, then they can know who and what you really are.

That advice is one of my earlier memories. My grandmother, with her big blonde hair, told me that many times. Her words, after her death, became more relevant and important than I am able to tell you.

She was called Martha and she was a singer in Romania under the communist regime. You may know it was led by the dictator Nicolae Ceausescu until the revolution that ended on Christmas Day 1989. Many people watched what happened that crazy day on the news. He and his wife, Elena, were insane people who destroyed the lives of millions. Nicolae was the monster who banned contraception and starved the hospitals of funds even as babies were affected with HIV by dirty needles. He was a monster who executed anyone he thought was his enemy, who had spies working for his secret police in every street, in so many private family homes, because he was so sick and paranoid.

And that winter the people said they had had enough of being watched and abused and killed, of having their families and cities and nation suffer because of the ego of this pig and his moron wife Elena. They ran for their lives but, I'm glad to tell you, they were caught and, on that Christmas Day, they were tried, then taken outside and shot dead. They died together and, when they put the film of their last moments on television, people across a whole country jumped for joy. Many laws changed after that, and one of the first was that capital punishment would be banned. They were the last people to be executed in Romania. I was six months old. I was born on 16 July 1989. Everything was changing in my country.

My grandmother sang for years, decades, in some of the top places in the country for the communists in the fifties, sixties, seventies. She had met some of the most high-ranking people in Romania. In her day she was an important voice in what was called the National Choir, which was owned by the country, by the regime she did not like at all. It toured around singing traditional folk songs for different crowds of people. Sometimes strangers would hug her when they saw her, they would tell her she was beautiful or would say that she could make them feel sad or wonderful inside. I was so proud of her.

And Martha really was a very beautiful lady, a very elegant person. But she was tough and headstrong and, growing up in the times she did, I think she only trusted about two or three people in her whole life.

I remember my mother telling me that a very important thing about her mother, Martha, was that, wherever she went, men always ran to hold doors open for her. And, she said, there was more to it than that. Because in the very unusual situation that Martha arrived at a door and a man was not holding it open, she would tell a man to open it – and the man would do so without question. I don't care if people open doors for me or not, but I love that my grandmother was a woman who had a standard that everyone had to respect.

My grandmother despised my own father, Stefan. She hated him because he and my mother fought all the time, because he was angry and violent and didn't have any love in his heart.

He was never a good choice in my grandmother's eyes, was never a good husband, never worthy of a woman as precious as my mother, and she was very right about that.

The truth is that Stefan never wanted to have children, never wanted to have a baby because he was interested only in money and, he said, it would cost too much to bring someone up in the world.

But he wanted my mother and I am sure that was only because she had some money, because she was from a better-off family and he could hide behind her drive to succeed in her life and wait for the rewards. My mother had proved many times that she was resilient and smart. She had tried many ventures in her life, often with enough success to make a little money, but never very much. In the days when I was a little girl, she was selling fish, a little business she had built from nothing. In the last years of communism, it was doing well.

Anna and Stefan were both 21 when they met but she was the only one who dreamed of making a nice home and bringing up a family. Before they married, he talked of taking her away on a lovely honeymoon and talked of Rome and Paris, places where it was so difficult for ordinary Romanians to go, and I think she always knew he was only telling lies. As expected, he never took her anywhere.

When she said she was pregnant, he told her the baby would not be welcome and something would have to be done. Abortion had been illegal in Romania for a long time, and an unwelcome baby, a baby that is not going to be recognised by the father, was called a 'baby from flowers', which means it would be thought of as nobody's child. My father told my mother that's what I was going to be. At least he was, for once, being honest.

My mother was upset but Stefan, you see, was not finished yet. He said if she gave him half of the money from the sale of her flat, which she planned to do after I was born, then he would recognise the child. The flat was all hers, had been given to her by her own parents, and he wanted half of it.

And, no, he was not finished yet. He also said he wanted me to have the first name of his choice because he knew that my grandmother was insisting, if I was a girl, I must also have the same name as my mother. And my poor mother did not know which way to turn.

In the end Stefan got his way with my name but, after disputes in the family, he was told he would not get half the flat, that it would stay in my mother's side of the family. And he was not happy.

I was a baby when he took me and disappeared. He put me in his car and drove almost 200 miles to the Hungarian border. He had been negotiating to get across when the police in Sibiu were told I was gone.

A search began and the border stations were contacted. It was discovered my father was seeking to bring me out of the country but had no identity papers for me and couldn't get through.

My papers, you see, had been hidden by my mother. I think her instinct had told her to assume Stefan might try to do something strange after I was born.

My grandmother had been sure, even before that time, that Stefan had a plan to get rid of me. She believed he would have been happy to abort me or lose me or even to sell me to criminals for any kind of price.

At the time my mother believed he was only trying to scare her, to force her into making a deal about the property she owned, that he was jealous of this new person arriving who was getting her love. She believed he had become confused.

I don't know what the truth is, but I can only say I'm glad he was stopped. After that incident, I am also glad to say, he was gone.

When I was four years old, I saw him again. It felt like it was the first time I was seeing him because of course I had no memory of what had happened before. But I remember being scared as he arrived at the flat with the purpose of attacking my mother. I watched with tears in my eyes as he hit her, as she tried to hide her face when he punched at her.

I didn't see him again until I was 17, and it was a short meeting. I arranged for us to meet because I wanted to ask him about those times. And you know, of course, he said what he wanted back then when I was a baby was to take me away to make a better life. He said things were too crazy in Sibiu with my crazy mother and grandmother and that he wanted to take me from all of that to make sure I had a better chance in life.

I asked him why he had hit my mother and he said that had not happened, that my mother had told lies about him and made them stick in my head like pictures on a wall. He said it could not happen because he was not an angry man.

I left him knowing that I did not believe a word he said and knowing that I never wanted to see him again. I had a strong sense of satisfaction, after that meeting, in knowing my own mind when it came to my father, in knowing that I was closing a door and that I would never open it again.

One of my earliest memories is of my grandmother telling me that, if I ever saw the man who called himself my father, I should run and tell her. I would have done exactly what she had said.

Some people don't have fathers in any sense that it means anything, and I am one of those people. But I had my grandmother, and I can tell you she was the finest parent I could have had. I loved her more than I have ever loved.

But Stefan didn't understand what it was to be a father. He was a man with a reputation in Sibiu, a man who fought a lot and didn't care what anyone thought of him. And, because of him, I was left with the name Sonia. It's my first name. My name is Sonia Anna, but you cannot call me Sonia, only Anna.

Do you know who Sonia is? She is one of the women my father was seeing when he was also seeing my mother. She is the woman he was with when I was a baby growing in the womb. And he called me Sonia, after her. Wasn't that such a nasty thing?

I was 15 when my mother told me about that name, about where it came from. I always hated it and then, suddenly, I had much more reason to hate it.

You can shout the name Sonia at me and I will not hear it. I will not recognise it. For you, my name is Anna.

So, yes, my mother and father split up after he was caught, after he had left Sibiu with me in his arms. My mother from then on worked hard and my grandmother was spending more and more time with me and taking me in most days of the week.

I didn't really live with my mother for very long when growing up, mostly with my grandmother. My mother was working hard at her business, but my grandmother was retired, and it made more sense that my grandmother would look after me. It made sense to everybody I think. It wasn't until she died when I was 16 that I moved back in with my mother, but only for a little while.

My mother had that little company, selling fish to shops, and she also did some bookkeeping for people when she could. But it was becoming a struggle for her. After communism fell everything changed economically and the truth is it worked out badly for her. And it's also true she made some bad decisions in her life. You know, some people are very strong, but not always in the best way.

In the end my mother became a nurse, going off to college in her forties so she could change everything for herself, and that's where she found what you might like to say was her calling, a place where she could use all of her strengths in the best way.

My grandmother's associations with the communists were strong on the professional level, but she always said in her heart she was a German. Her roots were German, she spoke German, her family being what are called Transylvanian Saxons, a people who settled in that part of Romania over hundreds of years right up to the twentieth century, and who speak German as their first language. She had many relatives, even close family, back in her beloved Germany.

Her people had a military background and she often daydreamed of what they had got up to and of returning to Germany, in the west, even though she had never been there in her life. She preferred not to have Romanian spoken in her house in Sibiu. I only ever spoke with her in German and I liked it that way.

By the time I was three years old my grandmother had given me a wonderful bedroom in her house and was taking me to the Hungarian-German kindergarten nearby. She wanted me to mix with children of German stock and to grow up being very sure of my identity.

Just like her I had this bright blonde hair, pure white, glowing hair, and she would tell me how beautiful it was and that it was part of the strong Saxon heritage I had in my blood. She loved all things German and things of high culture, like art and music and fine long dresses and beautiful food and flowers and jewellery and things that stimulated the mind and senses.

And she loved that I was her Anna, the same name that she had given to my mother, that she could call me her favourite word in the world, that I was another little girl for her to treasure.

Maybe for you this all sounds like a strange start to life, and I have to say I agree. But when you are very young, everything is normal. It was normal to be with my mother, when I was aged two or three, when she was crying. It was normal to pull her blankets over her when I was with her at weekends, for her to tell me that she had problems with people and had met only stupid men.

She lived in a flat in a block that had been built by her father, a well-respected project engineer. He built a lot of homes for the communist regime and, just as a gift to him, they had given him that flat when the job was finished. He passed it to my mother before he died.

It was on the corner of a busy street and you could hear cars going back and forward all the time. I found if I pulled the blankets over my head there would be a softer sound, much quieter. So if you had seen us, when she was upset in that flat, you would have seen my mother talking and wiping her eyes and you would hear the cars going past and hear her telling me she loved me. And you would see this little girl playing with toys under the covers in her normal world.

I liked being there with her, no matter what it might sound like. I liked hearing her talk. I had my own bed, a big double bed with a pink cover and stuffed with monkeys – I still love toy monkeys – but I so often liked to go and climb into my mother's bed and climb under the covers and let her talk and weep.

Sometimes she would try to keep me distant when she was crying, but then at times it was because I was with her that she cried.

I felt sometimes that I was the one who could stop her crying, that if I did nice things she would not be upset anymore, but usually that didn't work. If I drew her a heart and told her I loved her it would make it worse. And one time I picked her some wild flowers from the parkland near to her flat and, I can tell you, when I handed them to her it nearly broke her heart.

There were no tears at my grandmother's house. I can never remember her or me crying there. It was only joy – joy and excitement and conversations about the future and about moving ahead and becoming a young lady. For a little girl it was a wonderful place to be. She had a whole room for all her dresses, all handmade, and when I moved in that magic room became my room.

In her later years, after retiring in her sixties, she kept up her interests and ran her own little sewing company for a while. She was such an expert at stitching and making ladies' garments. After a while she decided it would be fun for us to be dressed the same and she and a friend of hers would make me dresses and skirts and tops to match my grandmother's clothes.

It was funny and lovely and kind of her to think like that. It gave me a real thrill to think people might think I had some of her class when they saw me dressed that way. I loved that, by the time I was five, she had my wedding dress picked out. It made me feel so confident, so secure about what the future held.

She taught me how to dance and, on so many days, we would whirl and glide around the house to her music and she would hum and tell me where to put my feet and to hold my head up. It was idyllic.

Her husband, my grandfather, died in 1985, in his fifties, so I never knew him. He spent a lot of his life in the Middle East, particularly in Syria, working with the government there and constructing huge office and apartment blocks. Some of what he created, I suppose, is some of what has been destroyed since Syrians went to war with each other.

He started working there in 1975 and came back a lot at first to Sibiu but in time, and as the work continued, he returned less and less and saw my grandmother less and less.

When he did come home, he often brought gold. In fact he sneaked it in among tools and official documents and boxes of sweets because he didn't want word to get out about it. My grandmother collected gold, wore it, enjoyed it and loved building up something that was not just beautiful, but precious. She loved unique things. She also kept it secret though. In those days, living in a dictatorship, spies were always talking behind people's backs, passing on information to the secret police, the corrupt Securitate. And the people who were doing well or securing valuable things from abroad would have been of great interest to them. They simply came round and stole from people all the time and there was nothing a person could do.

On one occasion, before I was born, the secret police searched my grandmother's house. They had been tipped off that there was precious metal there. They trashed the place, left it turned over like a storm had hit it. They had found some gold, something like a whole kilo in weight, and taken it away. But my grandmother was too clever to have made it easy for them to find it all. She always said it was her own friend who had tipped off the police and that was why it was so hard to trust people in this world. She told me she had never told that friend about the false compartment in the back of her wardrobe, and this was why they did not get all of her gold.

It's funny but, as I think about my grandmother, I can smell fresh bread and jam, my favourite smell in the world. I cannot stop associating her with bread and jam and I love it that way.

I would wake up in that big bed in that happy, colourful bedroom and there would always be bread and jam on the bedside table – fresh bread, fresh butter, fresh strawberry jam. Sometimes I would hear her coming in the morning and pretend I was asleep, just to hear her put the plate down along with a little glass of milk. I'd keep my eyes closed and listen to the noise and then, moments later, the smell of joy would reach my nose. The door would close and I would leap up and gobble the food.

She would then start the music. She played music almost all of the time, every day, and sometimes I could hear her singing quietly as she went about starting her business for the day.

My grandmother's house was three miles from my mother's but they were worlds apart. My grandmother's was a lovely house – not that my mother's flat was bad. But it's just that my grandmother's neighbourhood was quieter and, I think, a better place for children.

I was always happy there, being a little lady, having my grandmother put lipstick on me and fix up my hair before taking me for a walk.

Outside, in that area, most of the people spoke Hungarian, some of them spoke German and some spoke Romanian. My first language is German and it is Romanian too. I spoke them both from my earliest years. My grandmother disliked Romanian and my mother disliked German, which says something I think about their relationship.

I learned a little Hungarian too, and at school, as Romania worked to strengthen its ties with Europe, we were taught French, English and Spanish. I learned well, so if you want to talk to me in a language of your choosing, I will probably have a good idea what you are saying.

My best friend was a little girl called Mirela, one year younger than me, who lived just a few streets away. Her family had less than mine and I remember how I used to worry if Mirela was hungry, if she had enough to eat. But she would never complain about that – all she wanted to do was to see my grandmother's dresses, to see me in my latest wonderful creation. We could sit and talk about the stitching and material and colours for a long time. I think we both dreamed of spending our lives dancing around in fantastic dresses. We thought, I believe, that was what life could be about, that this was what my grandmother's life had been like. And of course, that was not at all true.

I was seven when my grandmother began trying to tell me life was not always pretty, that there were many bad things and bad people out there. My father, she said, was just one of them. She explained that, as a lady, I would find life very hard but how it was so important to always respect myself, never to stoop low to please others or to shame myself simply to get somewhere, to always reach high and aim far.

She would talk about these things and I didn't really ask many questions. I suppose I just assumed I would find out what she meant. We would talk and then she would read me a little Bible story and we would pray together. I only ever prayed in German.

When I was 14, as is the tradition among some families in the area where I grew up, I was given a gift of gold. For me it was earrings and a necklace from my grandmother. I remember that was a time when she again told me more about the world, about keeping only good friends, about avoiding people who make you feel unsure about their intentions. And always, she told me, always, always, behave and dress like a lady.

She never did get to move to Germany but, just once, in the 1990s, she did go to visit. Her brothers had managed to get back there during the communist era and, when the Berlin Wall came down and travel restrictions changed, she was able to visit and track down her own people.

But she came back unhappy, disappointed. She said her family had not welcomed her, that they made her feel as if she was an outsider in the place she had always wanted to be. They felt, she believed, because she had spent a career singing for the communist state, she was in some way more foreign than she would have been if she had lived a different life. It was hard for her, a cruel turn of events. All the doors would usually be opened for my grandmother, but here it was like one was closed in her face. It makes me sad to think she was treated like that.

In 2005 she became unwell, and I became unwell. It happened around the same time. She was diagnosed with leukaemia and I was diagnosed with pneumonia. It was strange that we both found ourselves being treated in hospital – her in the County Hospital and me in a children's hospital – at the same time.

The doctors found out I had allergies to some medications, to certain antibiotics, and it seemed to take them a while to really work out how to treat me. I had rashes and reactions and my body just was not cooperating. I looked like a red Dalmatian.

My fever went on and on and I remember times when I was lying in bed with the sweat just falling out of my skin, pouring out of me like I was melting. My temperature reached 43.5 degrees, which is very hard on the body. I can tell you they really did feel that I was getting close to death.

My mother read prayers over my bed and I listened, burning, not very conscious, thinking that this was it, the end for me. I thought I would soon know if there was a heaven and wondered what it would be like and what I would do there at my age and if I would be young forever.

They filled a bath with ice and cold water and took me to it. It was a last hope for them. I didn't really understand what was happening, but one moment I was in bed and the next moment I was being pushed and held in this terrible water.

I couldn't speak or think and just screamed, raging and in severe pain and feeling as if I was being tortured. It was the most horrible thing I had ever endured, but it worked. They got my temperature down to 36 degrees and I was told that I was lucky to be alive.

I was in hospital for weeks and weeks and had so many treatments and medications that my whole body was changed by it forever. I was told that the antibiotics they had to use – that they had no choice but to use – had damaged my ovaries. As far as they believed, I would have no chance of ever having babies.

This was just one more thing to upset me. I had never even had intimate contact with anyone and here I was being told I would never be able to have a baby anyway. My hopes for my future were falling apart.

My grandmother, I am sad to say, did not leave hospital alive. She needed blood transfusions, many times, as part of her treatment and her blood type was rare, Rhesus Negative A. It is my blood type too. I would have given her blood if it could have happened that way. I would have given her all my blood. But mine was full of drugs, it was the blood of a girl with fevers, and it would have killed her.

I saw her in her last days, when I was stronger, and there was nothing left of her. She was frail, small, just a twig. I prayed at her bedside, not for her to live, but for her to die and find peace. I knew she was struggling, that there was no hope, no return for her. I just hoped God would take her even though it was so hard to think of her not being in my life.

I found out she died in a phone call from Petre, who had become my mother's second husband. I remember thinking how she would be gone from that little room where she had spent so long, that it would be silent, that there would be just a little dent there, a small, shallow mark in the bed left by her from her last days. Her last little piece of trail from the journey she had been on. Losing her upset me so much, I cannot tell you.

I kept close to her body for three days, unable to sleep, uninterested in the world. I stayed with her coffin at her house, with my mother there too, and told her things when other people were sleeping.

She was 66 and could have lived for another 20 or 30 years if it had not been for the leukaemia, and I wish with all my heart that she could have done so.

I can tell you that a thousand people came to her funeral and a thousand people hugged me that day. I thanked all of them when they said they were sorry.

But I had never felt so alone in my life.

Chapter Four

I wanted to leave the country. Or, at least, I wanted a place of my own. I wasn't totally sure, but I needed to start moving along in life. I was 16 and was being told to live with my mother and this man Petre, who I did not like. Staying at my grandmother's house was not possible, even though I know she would not have minded that. But no, her family – mainly her two sons – wanted it for themselves.

So all I could do about this was what any teenager would do; I became grumpy and I let everyone know how I felt.

Petre resented me and I resented him. He wasn't the right man for my mother and she knew it. But that was her weakness – bad choices. He was always in a bad mood, even worse than me as a silly teenager. And he had a temper that I could not trust. I didn't really know where I was with him, where he was in his own mind. In all my times meeting him I never saw what I would call a kind man. A daughter gets an instinct for the right man for her mother, and this was not the man.

I threw myself into my schooling, really began to focus on using education to get me somewhere. I took up a dancing class and began tutoring younger students in mathematics because my grades had always been among the best in the city.

Mirela talked with me about Miss Romania. She knew I was down, depressed, trying to do something and to get somewhere but with no direction. She told me that, because of my body size and shape and my German blonde hair, I should go for the regional competition to see how far I would get. It seemed like a stupid idea. I had never thought about modelling. But maybe it was something that would be fun.

My friend's brother was my companion, the gentleman escorting the lady. It was in Sibiu, the regional heat for them to pick the girl who would be the representative for the area. And I won. I posed and pouted around on stage and walked and talked and smiled and blew kisses and did what they told me. And that was how I won.

It was exciting but not emotional, not in any way a deep experience. It's hard to explain. I remember being handed flowers on stage and thinking that this was lovely but not really that special. What did I do to deserve flowers? Flowers are for something better than pouting and smiling, I think. This was just a competition for girls who were being told to walk around and get looked at. In my heart it felt hollow, as if we were all pretending to be ladies, because we were not ladies.

I didn't go any further with it. I told the organisers the next time I met them that I would not be fighting to become Miss Transylvania, and then fighting on to becoming Miss Romania, and then fighting on to become Miss World. That little battle was over for me. I wanted something more. If I ever was to go down the route of appearing on a stage, it would be more about dancing than modelling, but even then I wasn't sure what I wanted to do.

I turned 17 in July 2006. It was a bad day. Petre came to my little room to talk with me about my thoughts about adulthood, about my plans for the future. He told me that, whatever happened, in one year I would have to be out of the house.

I said I didn't know what my plans were but I would keep him informed. I was expecting something from my grandmother's legacy but he said no one would get anything for a while as my uncles were fighting over everything. There had been no will, he reminded me, because she had not expected to die. He said I was too young to have any influence on what might happen with her wealth. My mother told me later that her mother had asked only that she look after me. Was that not her job anyway? I wasn't sure what I could believe. So my main problem remained the same – I had to get out of that house.

When school finished that summer, after my exams, I found a job in sales and they gave me a car to travel around from shop to shop. Food and beverages, you would call it. I learned to drive quickly, easily, and loved the feeling of independence. Believe me when I say I am, to this day, a good driver.

I stayed with friends on some nights and on other nights myself and little Mirela would drive around the city and smile and flirt and smoke cigarettes with some of the fashionable boys who spend their lives on city centre corners.

And on some nights I would sleep in that little car. I had folded-up sheets in the back and a pillow, and could wrap myself up and get cosy in there and no one troubled me. I would find silent places to pull up – car parks where no one was or alongside wooded areas out of town – and lie back and enjoy the silence, enjoy being warm and comfortable and thinking about my own place and all of my future.

As I said, one sideline I had taken on, maybe to avoid having to be in the house so much, was helping out in a dance class. I had waltzed around the house with my grandmother so many times that I had picked up different moves. But now I was learning more and putting into practice what I already knew by helping young people and older people who wanted to give it a try.

I loved those evenings, just swishing around and knowing that everything else in the world disappears with the joy of the movement. A tip for you – dancing is a happy thing and, even if you aren't happy, if you stand up and start swishing around in any room in the world you will find that it makes you happy. It is a chemical reaction inside, I think. Dancing, I think, is the body's way of smiling.

Sometimes I would look up the different dances, learning why they were called what they were called. To me that seemed more worthwhile than standing on a stage as a model, telling the world that I was a random someone who should represent them. It was much more comfortable for me to just move around a dance floor and not have a care.

Do you know I can dance 35 dances? Do you know I can tell you the story of them all? As far as favourites go, I love the Viennese Waltz – the grand, slow one, not the quick one – and anything classical. I can't dance so much anymore, not now that my back has been damaged.

I was almost 18 when I moved in with Alex. He was 27. And he was wiser and stronger and stranger than any man I had met before.

His family knew my grandmother and I knew she thought highly of them. In fact I had met him first through her as he lived across the street. But it wasn't until later that we began to see each other more and make something of our connection.

It was a strong tradition among some in that area that girls and boys should not be together, not in the physical sense or the living-together sense, until they were both 18. That's really how it was between us. We stuck very closely to the rules, although not entirely.

It felt lovely to be invited to move in with him, into his own flat near my grandmother's. And it felt totally natural too, a smooth progression after a few months of dating, a natural development without any questions in my mind. And, of course, it was also a relief to know I was going to be somewhere where I didn't feel unwanted.

The most unusual thing about his flat, and you would have noticed it right away, was that it had no decorations, really just a bed and some basic furniture, a few essentials in the kitchen. It told a story that he lived a simple life in a complicated world, or at least that he was trying to do that.

I would ask him why he hadn't got more things, more colour or art or little things that make him smile, and he said he was only interested in things that were useful to him. But he took my point. I did not have to say too much before he began taking me to shops to buy new bedclothes, paintings, decorations for the flat.

Just a month after I moved in he disappeared for three whole weeks. He told me he had some work to do, that it would involve him travelling and he would see me soon. I was there for all of that mostly on my own, cursing the paintings and the nice décor and the man who paid for it. When Mirela came round, we would drink wine and smoke cigarettes and talk about how much of an idiot he was.

When he returned, we fought. Or I fought. I demanded to know where he had been, what he had been doing, to make him understand how this had been for me, that I felt like a fool sitting around waiting, that I had better things to do.

But he said almost nothing in return. Then he told me he was crazy about me and we went to bed.

He told me he worked for different people as a representative. He said he was in sales, that he didn't want to talk about it. There was an arms factory some miles from our town where some Sibiu people worked and I remember wondering if he had something to do with that, if he sold guns, if he did something secret. He laughed and told me he had worked there and had friends there but that his life wasn't anything as exciting as I thought.

He took me to dinner, to see friends, to parties, to movies and sometimes we would just sit indoors and say nothing for hours. I liked it. I liked how he made me feel. It may sound crazy but I liked not knowing everything about him, I liked wondering.

And then he disappeared again, this time for a week. Then again, for a longer time. Then longer again. And all the time I had almost no idea when he was about to go and no idea when he would be back. There was a very occasional text message but most of the time he was completely uncontactable via phone.

*

The uncertainty, the insecurity, became harder and harder to deal with, yet when he was around he made me feel safer than anyone had ever done.

We talked about mathematics, about how problems have solutions, about cars and hair and buildings and history and how it's funny when people over- or underestimate people.

One night I was visiting my mother and I had an argument with Petre. It got a little bit out of control and I fell over, something between a shove from him and a trip by me, and I pulled some muscles in my back. I left there angry with him, but not surprised by the way he had behaved.

At Alex's house I had a shower. He came up to me as I was getting out, said he could tell something was wrong. I explained what had happened with the fool my mother had married. He nodded, kissed me, told me to wait.

A little while later my mother rang asking me if I had lost my mind.

'Why did you send this guy here?' she said, panicked.

I told her I didn't know what she meant or what was happening.

She said, 'Alex arrived with a gun and pointed it at my husband and told him he's going to shoot him dead!'

Petre was freaking out in the background, shouting. He was going crazy, saying, 'Tell her never, ever to bring that man back here. And tell her never, ever to come back.'

I had no idea Alex was going to do that. I didn't even know he had a gun.

He came back and I exploded like a bomb. I demanded to know about this gun and about why he did what he did, how he thought he could go and threaten my mother's husband, but as always he let me get my shouting done before responding.

'I made sure he will never touch you again,' he told me and put his pistol away into the bag he travelled with. 'You will be safer now. That is all I wanted for you.'

I wondered all night about what he did with his life. He was always able to support me with money, with words, with the love he showed to me.

But at the very same time he was a ghost, so often never there, never calling, never telling me anything about what he was doing.

One nice night we were together on the sofa, watching the movie *Memoirs of a Geisha* on DVD. I love that movie and had watched it many times, alone or with Mirela when Alex was away.

Alex and I were cosy, happy together in those moments and I just started to say some lines from the movie, a few words I didn't understand in Japanese that the geisha says to one of the gentlemen. And Alex replied, in Japanese. I don't know what he said, but the words were fluent, easy.

I sat up and asked how he knew those words. He said he knew a few words in a lot of languages, which was something he had never, ever mentioned to me. I tried him with a few words of French, English, Spanish and he was able to talk back in all of them. He wasn't fluent, but he had a good understanding. I told him he was always surprising me, always amazing me and always mystifying me.

*

Most people in Romania go into the army at 19 or 20. Some stay, end up working on different projects, or end up moving into the police. I told Alex that I thought it must be something like that with him but he said, 'No, I told you, I sell things for people.'

His advice to me was to join the police in Romania, then to try to move into SRI – the secret service – because he had heard there were good careers opening up there as my country shook off the past and became stronger.

I told him I would consider this, and I remember thinking how it seemed like a good idea.

Alex's parents were not well off but the area they lived in, my grandmother's area, was not cheap. I never did know how they had the money to live there. And Alex's own big flat was probably worth even more than his parents' house.

I said to him, 'Have you inherited? Are you an heir to someone's fortune?'

And he told me he was not.

Then he left for the last time. He told me the night before. He said he had to leave and might not be back for months. I knew what 'months' meant. If a few days meant three weeks then I knew what this meant.

I went after him in the morning, sad, crying, confused, hurt. But he put his hand up to me, a stop sign, told me I could go no further. Nobody knew he was going anywhere, not his parents, not his friends.

As the days went on I went to speak with one of his good friends, who told me he had no idea what was going on. I told him I wanted to make plans, that I could not sit in Sibiu waiting like a fool for this man. He said I should do what I had to do.

I called that same friend months later, just to see if he had heard what became of Alex. He said he didn't know but that his parents had been told he was in Asia.

I loved him, but he never came back.

Do you know what he told me? After that time he threatened to kill my mother's husband? He told me he would not always be around, that I had to be careful, that I must always be ready to protect myself.

He said, just like my grandmother had told me, that I should leave a trail, a path back to where I was before in life in case of taking wrong turns, a kind of escape route to the place where you were safe before. He said I should always leave evidence of having been somewhere. Knowing where you have been, he said, is as important as knowing where you are.

I told him I was not a silly girl, that I was no longer a princess swishing around in pretty dresses with no real clue of what the hell is going on in the world. And he told me to listen, to remember that, if I am going somewhere, I need to know how I got there. He told me to create maps and charts in my head, to remember roads, faces, dates, to find ways of remembering things and linking things together so I didn't forget them.

He told me I was a mathematician – just like him – and had a head for facts, that I should use those skills and teach myself to think at all times, that I should be more aware, that he felt I was more naïve to the world than I could imagine.

I gained more self-belief from him than I knew at the time. I heard the compelling case that the world can test you, throw you off track and that it is better if you are prepared, if you have some kind of escape plan. I knew from him that self-reliance is the greatest security you can find, that in all your life there is so little chance a protective, brave man will come to help you when you need it most.

I stayed in Alex's flat, kept working, saved up my money and began dreaming about leaving.

Chapter Five

I am interested in psychology. Understanding how the brain works is helpful when it comes to understanding why people do what they do. And there is nothing more interesting than people.

In the big picture, we all want the same thing – security, comfort, warmth, food, water, love – but what is in the small picture is how we get those things, the way we use them, the way we satisfy ourselves. That is where the distinctions are, the things that make us different. We all go down different roads to get to the same place.

I told my mother I wanted to study psychology and she said she was taking up nursing. There were vacancies for nurses, she said, and a good, local course was available that would ensure she got a job.

She told me I should think about doing the same. Psychology, she said, was probably very interesting, but I had to think about the future. I knew she was right in one way, that she was practical. And I knew, in my own stubborn mind, that I was also right, that reaching further was the first step to getting further. So I did both. I thought, if I do both, then I will be working towards becoming a medical professional. I will be, I said to myself, a psychologist. I found this very exciting.

I applied for a place on a three-year degree course based at Spiru Haret University in Bucharest. It was almost three hours away by car, but the full year added up to only 14 weeks over two semesters and I could do much of the studying from home. At the same time I took up a part-time place at nursing college. Both courses were publicly funded, so I had nothing to lose. But I was going to be busy.

It was a stretched situation, and perhaps a sign of my eagerness to move on at the time, but I felt committed. I would need to manage my time, my work and I would probably need to sleep in my car at times, but I was confident I could succeed. The nursing course was three years and maybe after that I could move to Bucharest, although that was not something I really wanted to do. So I began both courses in October determined to succeed.

I could tell you I wanted to do some good as a nurse, as a psychologist, and it would probably sound dishonest. But there was truth in that. I had been in hospital, I had been helped, saved, fixed by doctors and it did seem to me to be a wonderful way to make a living.

I was alive when I could be dead and I had to do something with my life, with the preciousness of being able to breathe and move and think as I wanted each day. Everything – in my head and my heart – pointed towards some form of career in working with people who needed help.

I did two years on the courses while working at the same time, earning around 800 euros a month, selling food and beverages and teaching a little mathematics to schoolchildren on the side. I was a good student, enjoying my studies and getting good grades and making new friends.

Most of the time I let myself into Alex's flat and stayed there, not really knowing what was going to happen with that place, unsure if he would ever return. His parents had been in to move some stuff around and, because I didn't really know them, it didn't feel too comfortable for me.

So I was also staying with my mother. We were both on the same nursing course and were both often sitting beside each other in lectures like old friends. It was good to sit around after classes and chat about what we had learned and the other people on the course.

One day I was at her house and went into the kitchen. Petre came to me and said, very simply, 'If you are going to be staying here again, you have to start paying full rent.'

I knew if he was saying it then it had probably already been discussed with my mother. Things had got tough for her too, with her doing so little work, so maybe it was understandable. My mother wasn't good at giving out bad news but this man was. He was very good at it. He enjoyed it.

I told Petre that I would help my mother out if she needed it whether I lived there or not. He didn't understand an idea like that. I asked him how much rent he was paying and he did not say. It happened to be zero. But, you know, his words had reminded me that I needed to get away from that place.

So there was a man I knew, a friend, a guy I had known on and off for a few years who grew up in the area of the city where my grandmother used to live.

We were the same age, knew some of the same people, and I had always liked him. You could say we came from different sides of the tracks as he was from a very poor family, but we had always had the same sort of mindset, an interest in the world.

He was called Marco and, when Romania joined the EU two years before this, he had moved to London. I was with a friend one day who was speaking on the phone to someone and she turned to me, held the phone out and said, 'It's Marco in London!'

We had a great little chat and he told me he was coming home to spend Christmas 2009 with his family and old friends.

'Anna,' he said, when we met, 'how are you? I miss the people from back home.'

We had a little cup of coffee and a laugh together. He told me about some of the work he had been doing, different jobs, and some of the places he had been.

'London's a big, big city,' he said, 'it's the biggest city in Europe, the capital of the world!'

Those words echoed in my head. I don't know why, but they meant something to me, something exciting. I had my hopes and desires, but for now I was thinking always about the future yet I was still in Sibiu and still, it felt, moving so slowly along.

On paper maybe it seemed like I was doing well, but there are times when you are young that you have itchy feet, that you feel things are not moving fast enough.

I met with Marco again over those holidays and he said he was looking forward to getting back to his life in London again. I told him I had been thinking about it, and the city and what it must be like, and he said he knew what I meant.

He said he was not legally able to have a job in the UK due to the 2007 treaty in place between the EU and Romania. It was difficult for him, he said, because he wanted to stay in London. If he had what was called a Blue Card, he said, he could work full-time and would make money, live legally and be much happier.

'I would have to be a family member of someone who had the right to stay in the UK in order to get a Blue Card,' he said.

For a moment I didn't see it coming.

And then he said, 'If we got married, just in secret, and you came to visit London for a while, I could get a Blue Card. You see, if you said you were a student studying in London, then you are allowed to live there with no questions. If I was married to someone who had the right to stay, I would be able to get a Blue Card.'

I said, 'What?!'

He said, 'Think about it, Anna. After one year, I would have the full right to stay like you would have. We could get divorced then. You would not even have to stay in London. Lots of people are doing this.'

I was hearing him fighting to make his point but he was not understanding what was going through my confused mind.

'Marco ...'

He said the treaty between the countries was 'transitional' and the Blue Card was just the current way of doing things.

'No,' I said, 'I am not asking you about the card. I am asking you – what? You are asking me to marry you?'

He opened his eyes wide and looked down at the floor. He said, 'Oh. Yes. I am. Will you?'

So that was unexpected.

Marco and I would never have been a couple in that way. But we had been good friends and he knew I was single, that he was not stepping on anyone's toes. And I am honest when I tell you

I am the sort of person who helps people out, who likes to do whatever I can when a friend comes calling.

We talked it over and looked it up and, after a while, I said, 'I accept your proposal.'

He said, 'Good. Apply for a passport.'

We could get married in a registry office very cheap. All we would need was two witnesses and to sign some forms.

There was a rule that said if we divorced within one year it would be free, and we only needed to be married for one year. In that time Marco could apply for the Blue Card and I could fill out some forms and go to where he lived in London.

It was exciting. I had a place to stay, I could look around, walk around this big city that so many Romanians before had not been able to see. He told me it would be no problem to work too, that I could easily pick up some jobs and make more money in a few days than I could make in maybe a month in Romania.

Within a few weeks, after I had finished my first-semester exams in January, I got prepared. I applied for EU student status through the university and was asked to pick some options in London. I had no idea about any of them, but I picked a few places that ran psychology courses and crossed my fingers.

And, very soon after, I remember putting on a nice, understated light-blue dress and getting married to Marco.

It was a funny day. The witnesses were two people he had asked in from the street about ten minutes before. We were both very concerned that our families would find out, so we were like secret agents with the information about our wedding. The only person in the world I told was Mirela, and I knew when I asked her to say nothing about this, she would respect that.

Myself and Marco had not thought how, as a matter of course, the marriage would be announced in the local newspaper. An official at the wedding told us that and said it was his duty to pass the details along. We could only laugh when we realised that sooner or later everyone would know Marco and Anna were husband and wife. I knew my mother was going to be stunned. But we were adults now and, we were sure, neither of us was a fool.

We married on 5 February.

The announcement was in the paper on the 17th.

The new Mrs Corbu left for London on the 15th.

I had accepted an offer to become a student at a university in London. A letter from them was enough for me to apply to live indefinitely as a student. I felt as if the world was opening doors for me.

In my pocket I had 1,500 euros saved from my work, from all of my life. And in my head I was thinking how all of this was going to be fun and interesting and daring and new.

Marco was living in a house on Pevensey Avenue in Enfield, north London, with 14 other Romanian people. We had a single room with no lock on the door, one little bed and we shared a toilet, kitchen, bathroom with everyone else.

It was crazy and busy and the ceiling over our room leaked when someone took a shower. It smelled sometimes and there was no space, but it was cosy in its own way. Marco worked very early hours and would sleep on the floor so I could sleep in the bed. I had had no illusions I would be moving to Buckingham Palace.

I liked hearing the stories people were telling me about living in a giant city and the places they had been and people they had met. And I liked even hearing how troubled things could get and how expensive things could be, about how easy it is to run into gangsters and run out of money. It was not ideal circumstances for anyone and many were having tough times, but we had all come from tougher times and we were making the most of what our parents could not. We were the first generation of post-communist Romanian people living in London and it was like we were reaching forward in the world and learning all the time.

Little groups would meet in the kitchen and drink beer and whisky and vodka, or hang out in bedrooms and advise each other about what we had learned or who we had met.

It is a strange thing but, when you want to get away from where you are, when you arrive you become so proud of where you are from. I laugh even now thinking how we would sing songs of our 'old country' while living in London. I tell you honestly that I loved those days. Identity is reinforced in those circumstances, my psychology tells me, and it feels important.

If I was going to be a student in London, I had months to spare before taking up my studies. All the time I was being asked about what I was going to do, how long I was going to stay. And all the time I was being told about lots of ways to make money, told how so many people were doing so well and saving up and also sending money home.

So I started looking around for jobs. I was able under what were called Yellow Card arrangements to work for 20 hours a week. It seemed to be foolish not to do this. Marco could go ahead and apply for his Blue Card, and I told him to make sure that he did. You see, I knew after a couple of weeks that he still had not got round to it. He was drunk a lot, took drugs at times and was not a wonderful person at organising himself and his time. To me, it felt as if he was partying on my time.

In my mind I was telling myself to make sure he did this one thing, as he promised to do, because the longer he did not have his Blue Card, the longer we would have to be married.

He had, he kept assuring me, an accountant friend called Jonny who would make sure his Blue Card came through.

At first I worked in a sandwich bar, making up food and cleaning tables. A girl at the house had given me the name of the owner and I had approached him, asking if there were any hours for me, and he said that would be fine. It wasn't very interesting but it gave me enough to make sure I wasn't just wasting cash doing nothing.

One Romanian girl I had a coffee with, when we were closing up one evening, told me that the money for working in the sandwich bar was very bad for London. When I agreed with her, she said she knew some girls from our country who had other work, who were making much more money.

'What do they do?' I asked.

'You know,' she said, 'sex.'

'Ah,' I said, 'they can't be happy.'

The girl shrugged at me. She smiled, she said, 'Happy with the money maybe.'

It was not the first time the subject had come up. I was hearing of the explosion in the numbers of east European girls working as prostitutes in London, of how they were being advertised like clothes or cars on the internet, how the men were paying only in cash, that in such a big city the supply was never greater than the constant demand.

I told my friend in the sandwich bar that I couldn't do something like that, no matter what money was being paid.

When March came I had to make decisions about college. Was I going back to Romania, was I staying in London to begin my course there?

There was not too much waiting for me back home. There was not a happy family or a wonderful job or life where I felt in my heart I really should be. What I did have was a different life, a life where I was making connections and making money and where I was, even so far from home, feeling happy. This new world was good for me, I could feel it.

So, to avoid regrets, I would stay longer in London. I would stay until May, work until then, save some more money, then decide if I was to be a student in London or in Romania.

I kept my mother informed – she never quite got over my getting married – that all was well. I told her I would soon start sending her money home as long as she would promise to me she would not tell Petre.

When May came, I was no longer a person who wanted to be a psychologist or a nurse or a student of any kind. I was finding out that I was a hard worker, that I took early nights and started early in the morning to get to my work. I was ticking like a clock, imagining that if this was where I was beginning then I could make much more of myself. I liked having possibilities, making decisions and did not like the idea of drinking all night and taking drugs and losing what was an opportunity. London, I knew for sure now, was right for me.

I made sandwiches and I served pizza. I worked for a time in a laundrette, in a coffee shop and an Indian restaurant, and all of those were legitimate and I was what I wanted to be – a taxpaying individual. I had lots of jobs, a few hours here and there, and I would wake up happy most of the time.

One of the women in the house ran her own little business cleaning houses and asked me if I wanted to help. This one was off the books and would pay me £30 a day for easy duties. I said that would be fine.

This was not great work. Cleaning homes for people who are lazy or who need help or whose houses were too big for them to look after was not an exciting thing. It was not something I had ever done much before but, as I had been told, it was not complicated. I got on with it not because I had to, but because I had a drive inside me that said I was going in the right direction.

The worst part was having my cleaning work inspected by this woman, who did almost nothing, who asked me to do it all. She sat around on her phone and then took all the credit for being really industrious.

When the householders were not around, she would hint in her own rude way that I wasn't so great at my work. She would laugh and suggest it, as if that made it okay to say. That really annoyed me. I was good at what I did. We were not going to be lifelong friends. I thought many times, 'I will walk away from this woman tomorrow – I don't have to do this.'

It wasn't long before I found out she was earning £100 a day even though she was giving me just £30. I heard her having a conversation in English with one of the customers. That made me feel like a fool.

That summer I went back to being in two minds about going home. I was bored with much of what I was doing every day and felt a little guilty about leaving my mother for so long, even if it was what her husband wanted.

I checked with Marco about his Blue Card. I wanted to make sure we were not going to be tied together for too long, that he would be able to hand me back all my papers now that they had been put into the application process. I had remembered he had not yet returned them.

'Everything is in the room,' he said.

'Where?'

He did not know.

'What is going on?'

He had been a fool. He told me he had not yet applied for his Blue Card, that he had been so busy working and had too many late nights, but that his friend Jonny would fix it very quickly.

'So where are my papers now?'

He just shrugged again.

Had they been stolen from our room?

This was the moment when I really became the odd one out in the house, because I started to cause problems. I asked every single person, more than once, if they knew anything about my passport, my marriage certificate?

Nothing came of these enquiries so I asked again. I can be forceful like that.

'Who has got my papers?' I said, to everyone, a few times, many times.

But no one knew, or no one admitted knowing.

I felt stupid, annoyed, maybe even sad at this situation. I was being messed around by someone, by a thief or an idiot, and I will not suffer people like that for too long.

I put everything to the side of my mind to think, to see if I could work out who had stolen from me.

An idea came. I sneaked a look at Marco's phone. I looked up the number of the man called Jonny.

I said, 'Oh hello, I'm Marco's wife Anna and I believe you might have spoken with him about a Blue Card?'

And Jonny said, 'Yes, it's nice to speak with you, Anna.'

Jonny said Marco had only just given him the papers a few days before. It would take maybe one to three months before a Blue Card could be received.

So I had been lied to. He had forgotten to do his application and, when I wanted my papers, it was then he said he did not know where they were. He took them and gave them to Jonny.

'Well,' I told Jonny, 'there has been a mix-up. I am applying for a Blue Card, not Marco.'

'You are a student so you can have a Yellow Card,' he said.

'I am a student and I have been working for five months on a Yellow Card. Is there any reason I cannot apply now for a Blue Card?'

'Anna,' he said, 'I can get you a Blue Card.'

'Good,' I said.

Had Marco paid him? No, and he had been hoping that Marco would pay him upfront. So I told him I would pay him the next morning, and I would pay him £100 and not the £80 he was hoping to get from Marco.

'And all of this is fine with Marco, by the way,' I said. 'He has just got too many problems at this time. The application should be for me.'

In August, one nice warm day, there was a party in our house and I joined in the fun. One girl told me there had been some post earlier. I went to the door and looked around, found the envelope. It was my passport, my marriage certificate and a Blue Card dated 6 August 2010. I was delighted. I was excited. I was jumping for joy. Whatever I was going to do now, I was holding in my hands my right to work, to stay, to do as I pleased in the UK.

Marco had no idea what had been happening. I went to him as he was drinking beer and talking to someone. His eyes were blurred as this man, my husband, tried to focus on me.

I said, 'Look, I have got a Blue Card.'

This was a shock to him. How did I have this? Where was his? How did I have my passport? He nearly spat his beer out. The reason he married me was to get this, but here I was holding my own in front of him now.

'Where is mine?' he said.

'I don't know,' I said. 'Talk to Jonny.'

'You bitch,' he said, 'where is mine?'

'Talk to Jonny,' I said.

It was not going to be nice staying with Marco any longer and now, of course, I was free to do what I wanted to do. I was married only in name, not in my heart. In my heart I was single, young and fit and free.

I flew back to Romania to see my mother. Did I still want to be a nurse? She asked me this many times, and I said I didn't want to bury myself in studies.

I told her some of the people I had met were snakes, but that I had no job in Romania and I had a Blue Card for London. I said I was going to go back and start my own little cleaning business, just like the woman who ripped me off. I would be getting divorced from Marco, I said, and my head was just getting clearer all the time.

Petre asked me all about what I was doing and I told him things were fine. He said he was glad I was doing something that was working out. He said he knew a friend who was hoping to move to London and asked if I could help. I told him I didn't think so because I was going to be busy.

Chapter Six

I moved into a house in Wembley with a Turkish lady and set about putting little cards into the windows of shops in north-west London.

'Experienced cleaner,' I wrote, 'references available, prices negotiable.'

I'd never thought about being a cleaner before I left for London, but I knew something about it now. It was a start for me, a way I could begin on my own, and I valued what I had learned.

Nothing happened fast, but over time, over a few weeks, more by word of mouth than by advertisement, I managed to build up customers. Most seemed to like me, to have faith in me and my work, and that felt good. Doctors, lawyers and all sorts of people in all sorts of interesting properties.

And in very little time some of them were handing over keys so I could come and work there even if they were not around.

My patch, if you want to call it that, was the area of north Finchley, Finchley Central, Golders Green and Kilburn. Some of the people there were so rich, with beautiful homes filled with beautiful things. And others were rich too, although had less beautiful things. Some were not rich at all, but they needed things cleaned.

Sometimes at night the Turkish lady would try to teach me words in her language and we'd chit-chat about the news and the weather and the people in England and the price of things in London. It was very civilised and I liked it. I was happy there. I was always sober, always ambitious when I was in that place. I am the sort of person who maybe lives in her own head a lot, who likes to let her mind drift away to silly places, who is maybe a bit of a loner. And, because of all of that, the house and the job were perfect. I was free, happy, Blue Carded and keeping money aside to pay my taxes, so I did not even have any guilt about that. I had no one to answer to and no one was causing me any problems with me being just me.

The Turkish lady hated asking for money, hated when it came to the end of the month and I would give her the rent. She was always saying 'Sorry' and that it was nice to have me in the house and all of this, but I would tell her all the time that it was fine, I owed her the money and that I was doing okay.

She told me her daughter was coming back in December and that she would be going away again in January, and I said all of that was fine. I was going home for Christmas 2010, I said, and still I was not sure if I would come back to London. I was always keeping my options open, I said.

Things at home did not go well. My mother and Petre went off to visit his sister for the festivities, as had been their plan, but they did not make arrangements for me to have access to the flat. I arrived in Sibiu late and they had already gone. I called my mother and Petre, who liked to answer her phone, told me I should look up some friends and not expect to have the use of my mother's house all the time. I had not been sending much over from London, he said.

I did not get on with him or his family and the way I think of it is that he and his family poisoned my mother against me. She was controlled by him and it drove me crazy. In fact, she drove me crazy. He drove me crazy. It felt like all of the country was poison to me when I saw the reality of what was going on with my mother. I was hurt so hard at that time that I just wanted to run away and never see my mother again.

I had sent her £150 just a few days before but it counted for nothing. I am sure Petre took it straight from her, much as every man had taken things from her in her life.

And what now, I thought, about my grandmother? What of all her estate, all her gold, all the things she left behind? If you asked me to guess about that, then I would point you towards my two uncles and Petre. They had been battling it all out since she died.

I was so unhappy. I called my old friend Mirela and said, 'You will not believe what kind of welcome I have just received.'

She said, 'Anna, come and stay with me and my family for Christmas.'

Her mother hugged me when I arrived. I knew she felt my family was a mess.

I can tell you that time felt like the blackest part of my life. I sank into a deep depression after deciding I had no home in Romania now. I felt I had cut ties without meaning to cut ties. I could have walked off a cliff that Christmas if I had been near a cliff. Instead, I spent some good times with Mirela and, I will be honest, we drank too much.

This wasn't like her, nor like me. I'm not much of a drinker. I am not someone who takes drugs. I am not a person who ever wants to be out of control or have control taken from her. But on this occasion, in a house where they had a lot of alcohol, I drank a lot of alcohol. Beer, vodka, wine, you name it.

Mirela's mother called my mother on the phone and they had a fight about all of this, about the state I was in and the unhappiness she had been able to see in me. Can you imagine how that felt? She told my mother that she had no excuse for behaving as she had behaved towards me, and I knew that was true. I had to go back to London. And I must tell you I had brought Christmas presents for my mother and Petre, which I left at Mirela's house for her and her family instead.

Mirela asked me if I was sure I wanted to go back to London and I said I was. I think she knew this really was a turning point for me and I suppose we felt like we might not see each other again.

I can tell you that, to this day, Mirela says that is the worst thing she ever did, that she did not make me stay in Romania, with her and her family, and never return to London. She still tells me how sorry she is that she was the person who, as she feels it in her heart, let me go to London in 2011.

I moved back to the Turkish lady's house and contacted all the people I had been working for. I was determined to be extra busy, to move forward on my own and save money.

In time I was working 20 houses a week, talking with homeowners and getting to know their pets and their habits and asking them to spread the word about me. It became my only job – cleaning. And I was good at it, I had the temperament for it. No dirt could survive my angry efforts to get rid of it. And people referred me to other friends and more calls came. I was in business.

Soon I had dogs and cats who were like my own pets and I was working in wonderful houses like they were my own offices. If you had seen me you would have seen me with an iPod playing into my ears every day and I would have been singing along and, day by day, making a life for myself.

Three weeks after moving back into the house in Wembley, I moved again, to Wood Green. The Turkish lady, so politely, needed the room for her family and this was fine with me. It was very understandable.

I moved to a big shared house, which was, like the first house, full of Romanian people, maybe as many as 15. I was paying less rent and it was closer to where I was working. I had taken a room of my own and it was comfortable, being surrounded by Romanians from all over. Maybe it was a bit like being at home, or being with a family, and that was perhaps what I needed at the time.

The landlord himself was Romanian and lived in one of the rooms. He gave me little bits of details about who was living there, who was coming and going, about who did what and who was from where. He said, as someone who owned the house, he often worried about what people got up to, but that the police had never yet called at his door. He was joking, I think. But he did say that I should keep my eyes open, that some people came from Romania with bad intentions, or got caught up with bad people, and I should be careful.

I got a phone call from a friend of Marco's and it wasn't good. He had been staying with a man, a friend of Petre's from Sibiu.

The man had moved over with his son and had just told Marco that his cousin was now coming to London and he needed the space. Apparently Marco was desperate for help, had nowhere to go and was just about to start a new job.

'Marco will end up on the street,' his friend said, 'because I cannot help him.'

I knew what he was asking. I asked why Marco had not called me himself, and he said, 'You know why – he is ashamed.'

Everything had fallen apart for him, the man said. He had made some mistakes – drink and drugs and money – but was now turning things around. He asked me if Marco could stay, just for a little while, two weeks at the most, in that house. I was, he said, his last chance.

I didn't think too long about it because, in a way, I felt sorry for him, my husband. He had made problems for himself and was paying the price, but I knew he was a nice guy. Marco took too long to get round to things, took too long to pay back money he owed to people, spent too long lying in bed after drinking too much vodka and smoking too much dope. And the more he did these things, the more trouble he found himself in.

'I won't make him sleep on the street,' I said. 'But no parties, no one else must come round, no making a fool out of me.'

The week he moved in he started working nights as a dumper driver in Stratford. By the time he got home each day, I was usually gone. Sometimes he would not come home at all and that was fine with me. But if I was still there when he arrived, he would not disturb me or trouble me. He slept on the sofa and was quiet, respectful. I felt sorry for him.

The landlord asked me about him and I explained it was a favour for an old friend. He was nice about that. He said strangers were more of a concern to him than friends when it came to meeting people in London.

He then said he didn't like one of the couples upstairs, Carol and Crina, that he didn't trust them. She's a stripper, he said, and they have friends who run prostitutes. He said they sometimes had a lot of money, sometimes none at all.

'Okay,' I said, but I had not really seen this couple.

'Not good people,' he said.

Four weeks later, outside that house, I was taken.

Some girls are tricked into coming to England or Ireland or Spain or Germany. Some are told they have a job waiting for them but then find out, on arrival, what the job really is.

Some have run up debts with people who bring them from countries like Romania with the promise of accommodation and security, and they have to work off the debt.

Some are tricked into thinking they are loved, that a man is going to make everything wonderful for them if they just help him out in this way and that way.

Many are fed lies and distortions and exaggerations and nonsense for weeks, months or longer before they find themselves too far out of their depth, and they end up telling themselves they have to comply, that it's all their own fault. It can be a many-layered and complicated thing.

But in some cases, in more cases than you might believe, the women are just taken. They are carefully selected and then swiped off the street, out of houses, from cars, and put to work. And it does not take too long before minds and beliefs and knowledge can be pulled apart like a ball of wool, before bodies can be battered and damaged like teddy bears in hurricanes of glass and stones. If you lose track of yourself, your physical self and your mental self, you lose track of everything.

And that is my story. I was four weeks from being beaten and raped and beaten and raped and raped and raped again. I was four weeks from becoming someone's property, someone who would value me at 30,000 euros and put me up for sale. This was all about to begin in Ireland, a country I am not sure I could have shown you on a map.

Chapter Seven

We drove to Luton Airport. I had been there before, to fly to Bucharest. I had never really been comfortable with what lay ahead when I arrived at Luton Airport. As we drove in I began to consider that I was being taken back to Romania, but why would they do that?

We pulled over in a car park.

Crina the stripper said, 'Do what you are told. Do not dare do anything else.'

She got out and opened my door. She told me to get out. Carol came alongside me and waved for me to follow him. As soon as I began walking, he walked beside me, then fell back a bit, a little behind me. Behind him were Crina and the driver, who left at some stage. It was as if I was leading them somewhere.

We walked into the airport and Carol, speaking low behind me, moving in close behind me, said, 'There' and 'Go' and 'Over there.' He was directing me to the check-in area. Soon I realised there were just two of us, Carol and myself. He was maybe 35, tall, broad, unshaven, wearing a black hoodie and tracksuit trousers and trainers.

'Walk,' he said, 'psst – go, walk, walk, walk.'

He smelled clean, not of drink or cigarettes, of the things you might expect to smell on some crazy kidnapper. He smelled as if he had been looking after himself. I didn't know him at all, but I knew he was Roma, from an ethnic minority in my country.

'Go,' he said, 'walk, walk, walk, walk, move, move, move.'

There was no queue when we arrived at the desk. There was no one at all but for the lady sitting there, smiling at us. Carol put the documents, mine and his, onto the desk. We had no bags. The lady lifted them and looked at them for three seconds and passed the documents back. She passed us two boarding cards.

'Thank you,' she said, but neither of us said anything.

'Walk, go, walk, move,' he said, pressing behind me, driving me forward.

I looked around and no one in the world was watching. There were cameras everywhere but why would anyone be watching us? I looked at them, at people, at anyone I could see, but why would anyone look back? How would anyone know what was happening?

My mind was smoother now, calmer, a little more controlled than it was confused, although I was still very confused. It was telling me now that only I could deal with the problem. But at this point I didn't know how big or small this problem was. I was in a no-man's-land in terms of what I knew.

'Move, move, move,' he said. 'Psst,' he said, 'go, move, move.'

I had no other words, no other ideas. I could see that he kept looking behind, as if at someone, maybe at the others who had been with us, and then back to the front again.

We walked towards the security people. A man looked at me and I saw him reach out. I looked into his face and he looked into mine. He didn't smile.

Carol reached in front, handed him the boarding passes, and the man looked at them and handed them back.

'Go through please,' he said.

'Move, move,' said Carol.

I could feel him right behind me, touching me, maybe trying to look as if we were a couple travelling together.

'Your coat,' he whispered to me, and I knew what he meant.

I removed it, placed it into a box on the conveyer belt and stepped forward, ready to be searched.

A lady waved me forward with a smile.

I walked through an archway and out the other side. My phone was in my coat. It came out the other end of the conveyor belt with no problem. I collected my coat and Carol collected his.

'Go,' he said, 'move, move, move.'

I could not read the signs, the boards, the information. But I know now we were going towards a stand for the Luton to Galway plane, flying with Aer Arann.

Carol's hand gripped the back of my elbow and I moved forward.

'Move, move,' he said, 'go, move, move.'

When I think now about those moments, I don't blame myself for walking forward, for going where he wanted me to go. It was a strange, surreal thing that was happening to me and I didn't know enough to come up with a different way of behaving.

I think even that if someone had come up to me and said, 'Is everything all right?' I might have said, 'Yes, everything is fine, thank you.' It is how I was managing it at the time. I was controlled when maybe I should have been uncontrolled. I was being cautious when maybe I should have had no caution. But at the time I had no idea what lay before me and every time I tried to make sense of it, to come up with answers, I became confused again. And all the time that I was building up theories in my mind, I was moving forward, further and further into the situation they had drawn up for me. Yet I was still in an airport, still on dry land, still in what I thought of as being a safe place. It was never clear in my mind when, or how, I should get help but I knew there was hope.

Do you know what was clearer in my mind? Crazy things, things that had nothing to do with my immediate problem. Was this a way of dealing with it? I looked at signs for cafés and at people eating and thought how hungry I was, how very, very hungry I had become. Then I was thinking about thinking about being hungry, that how even though my stomach was light and nervous and full of butterflies, it was telling me it was empty. I thought about my mother, what they had said about her, about the blunt threats they had made, if she was okay. And I thought about my job, the house I was due to clean that same afternoon, how there would be disappointment because I did not show up.

We sat in the departure lounge for about 20 minutes, some people coming in and sitting down and reading their papers and their phones. There was one old couple who moved very slowly, who smiled at everyone and whispered to each other all the time about the other people there. I wondered if they had anything to say about me and this man.

But there were not many people, maybe just ten, maybe twelve, something like that. And when we were called I saw through the window that this was a tiny plane with propellers, not big turbines like a jet.

Walking on board, going through the door of the plane, I still felt as if there was hope. It may sound crazy but I had no big reason to think my life as I knew it was ending. I had moved from an airport to an aeroplane but still there were people all around me who could help.

I took my window seat at the back and the man sat a seat away from me. There was no one close to us. They locked the door and the lady showed us what to do if we found ourselves in water and I was telling myself that a crash might not be a bad thing for me. I looked out as the loud propellers spun and the plane raced along and took off into the air.

I wondered if maybe they had taken the wrong person. And then I thought how they had already bought a ticket in my name, that they were sure I would be getting this flight. How could they be more sure of where I would go that day than I was?

It was like something from a bad dream, watching the world get smaller below us. Maybe it was no worse to be with this man in the sky than it was to be with him on the ground? I thought how when we got to where we were going then it would maybe be no worse being with him there than it was being with him in London, or being with him on that plane.

I felt I was far from where I wanted to be but in a funny way that the situation was not getting more dangerous. This was not his plane. I told myself, in so many ways, over and over, he was not in charge of everything around us. This would not be his airport, or his streets when we landed. A little stupid part of me said that I could walk, or run, at any time. I reminded myself that I was not as scared as I had been. And, you know, that is what amazes me when I think back. I had started to adjust so well to what was happening that I was able to accept the unacceptable.

The captain spoke about flying to Galway and I didn't know where it was. I didn't hear everything he said because my ears were full of the noise of propellers and popping with the change in the thickness of the air. But it was the first time I had heard the word Galway and I didn't know where it was.

Carol said, 'Don't cry. No, no. No fucking crying. No, no.'

And I was crying, tears running down my cheeks, tears from muddled and scared and stupid thoughts. Tears of a girl trying too hard to be clever, too hard to be strong, and letting her life get stolen from her in the same minutes.

We did not speak again on that journey. After an hour, we landed. We waited for the other passengers to get off.

And then, 'Up, move. Up, move, move, this way, now, now.'

My eyes were wet as I was smiled off the plane by a stewardess. We walked down the steps and into a little airport that looked like a bus station. There was no one there to check us, to inspect us. I will tell you that again – there was no one there watching who got off that plane. No one checking tickets, passports, baggage, anything. So we walked into Ireland.

Two men, one tall and fat, one more normal-looking, walked towards us, looking up and down at me – up and down and up and down. I knew then it was make or break. I was with one, but in seconds I would be with three. I had to shout or run or fight now, right now. Now was the time. This was my last chance.

The fat man reached out and took my hand. They both smiled. No one looked me in the eye, not for more than a split second. They started to talk, but not to me. They talked about me.

'This is nice,' said the fat man. 'She looks good.'

And what had been at the deep and dark back of my mind was now at the very front in clear daylight. These were pimps and I was the girl. I knew, with no doubt now, I would be raped by someone at some time. My instinct was shouting it at me. The future was already sure.

But still I was frozen, scared to speak. Here I was, two hours into this nightmare, and I was saying nothing, not even interrupting them.

Let me introduce you.

The fat man is Vali. He is ugly, sleazy and he would rape me.

The other man we met is Ilie, or John as he was known. He stinks of cologne and wears Adidas tracksuits, expensive watches and gold rings.

And the man who had brought me there, Carol, is the small fish among them. He would rape me too.

You know what is funny? Their car broke down as they drove me towards Galway City. I was sitting in the back with two men who were taking me to I don't know where so that I could be raped, and their car started chugging. Vali pulled over at a petrol station and cursed in anger over and over again. The other two insulted him, laughed at him as he got out to look at the engine.

I think I maybe hoped this was as if the world was telling me I was not supposed to go where I was going. But I was between two men on the back seat of a car in a place I did not know, so it was not as if the world was going out of its way to help me.

'He fixes his own car all the time and won't get it done properly,' Ilie said.

And he said it to me, as if we were friends, as if I had an interest in the life of this man who was driving me down a road I did not want to be on.

I didn't say anything.

And then I said, 'Where am I going?'

And neither said a word. My voice was nothing to them, not even a sound.

Vali closed the bonnet and got back in. He tried the engine a few times and it started up. He revved it loudly as the men insulted him over the noise, and off we went again.

'Overheating,' he said, when it became quiet again. No one said anything.

It was getting darker but I could see the sea now, just as we started to come into Galway. At first I thought it was a lake but then I realised we were right on the coast. I knew we had flown over water already, and I knew then this must be the Atlantic Ocean.

The car pulled up on a street in a part of the city called Salthill. They got me out and walked me along a pavement towards a betting shop. Here they seemed to be slowing down. They walked just past it, to a doorway that led to the flat above. One of the men opened the door and pushed me inside, into a dark stairwell. It stank of dirty air, of dirty walls and floors and doors and people. I walked up first, all three behind me, and I knew this was it, where I was going to find out everything. This was where, I was sure, I was going to be raped.

The door at the top was open and a woman in a red robe and flip-flops came towards me.

'In there,' she said.

The men were right behind me. I felt as if they were going to push me forward. I turned left into the living room. They all came in afterwards and closed the door. I stopped, looked around, turned to see them all.

She slapped me. It took two seconds for me to hold my face and think about what had just happened. I held my hand up to my face. She hit my hand away and slapped me again. And again.

'Don't hide from me,' she said, and slapped my face again. Then my head, my ear, then my face again. I pulled back, hands over my face, screamed, 'Stop it!'

It stopped and I would not look. My body was shaking, every muscle, every limb shuddering with rage and fear. I looked, maybe through my fingers – I can't remember – and the men were just watching.

Her name is Ancuta Schwarz. She is short and ugly and makes the sound of flip-flop wherever she goes. She has this long dark hair that she likes to toss around as if she is a princess. She is evil and vicious. She is self-obsessed, hates everyone on earth and is jealous of everyone on earth. She is, in the world as I have known it, the most messed-up person on the planet.

'Sit down,' she said. There was a wooden chair behind me. I sat, shaking like a leaf. One of the men went to a computer; the other two were chatting about something to each other.

Ancuta looked to them.

Around me I saw a room full of phones and laptops. It was a room with a light on and the blinds closed on both windows.

It had a sofa and a table. There was a kitchen area, some kitchen chairs, a fridge. There were dirty dishes and rubbish. It had a wooden floor. No TV. The air was full of smoke, of alcohol, of sweat. It was dirty air.

The man at the computer was telling another man about some cocaine. Another girl walked into the room, closed the door, looked at me like I had said something to her. I looked away. She was 17 or 18, thin as a stick, wearing a bra and jogging bottoms.

Ancuta picked a cigarette out of a packet on the table, lit it and smoothed her hair back, flared her nostrils and blew out the smoke. The girl reached for a cigarette too. Ancuta looked as if she was preparing for something.

'What do you want?' I said. I don't even remember if I planned to say it, but out it came.

Everyone looked at me. It was as if they had just learned I had a voice.

'Take your clothes off,' Ancuta said.

I looked at her, my face straight.

'Take your clothes off,' she said, firmer.

And she stepped forward. She slapped me. Then a punch to my chest. Then a pull on my hair, as my face was in my hands.

Ilie stepped over, grabbed me by an arm, pulled me closer.

'Listen,' he said, 'you listen!'

Maybe I was too terrified to fight, or maybe I was just not fast enough. In a split second they were pulling at my coat, my trousers, my T-shirt. In an instant I was on the floor and they were pulling at my underwear. In no time, in maybe four seconds, I was bare. They pulled me to my feet and I felt as stupid and scared and fragile as I had ever been. Only my arms could cover me. It is crazy now when I think how I tried to not let them see my full body.

As they stared, I felt myself going downwards, the strength vanishing from my legs, going to the floor, curling up. And slaps came. Slaps to the head, the face, the nose, the ears, my back.

I could not look at them. I wanted it to be as if I was not there and they were not there. But I could hear them talking, chatting, as if this was nothing strange. I heard no words from that other girl, just Ancuta talking about this 'blonde bitch' and 'blind bitch' on her floor.

I wanted to die. I spent a moment, maybe more, working out if all of this was real, and when I knew it was, when I went through the sequence of memories of the last two or three or four hours, I wanted my heart to stop. Whatever it took, this had to end.

Someone pushed my head down, banged it off the wooden floor. They pulled it up again by the hair and banged it down again. I don't know if I screamed or how much I was crying. I can't tell you. I have no idea how or maybe even if I was coping.

A phone rang, a low buzzing, and I heard the girl I knew only as Bella. She was chatting nice and friendly to whoever it was in English.

'Yes, baby,' she said, and she had the voice of a child to match her body. The call ended and she spoke to Ancuta in English.

Ancuta said, 'Hey, blind one.'

And I could not look up.

Slap.

'Blind one!?'

I opened my eyes and looked up to see her blowing out smoke. Her face was blurred, a light bright above her.

'You are going to meet your new boyfriend,' she said, in English.

Those were fearful words. I felt as if some angry words might come into my mouth in return, but I said nothing. My lips were stinging. I knew they had become swollen.

A phone rang, a different ring, and the girl answered again in English.

Ancuta told me to stand, then to sit on the chair. And I did, my head down, my arms over my breasts.

I looked at the floor, at my bare feet on the dirty wood. I closed my eyes and tried to think of something that might help me. I thought about what I had to do, how to get away from this, how to stop it, and I had no answers. But I believed that this could not last too long, that there would be some kind of time limit on this.

I remembered my mother's face, I remembered I was so, so hungry, somehow more hungry than I had ever been. I thought how I was thirsty, that if I could eat and drink now it would make me strong again. These were maybe irrational thoughts, but thinking them was some small way to block out everything else in my head.

Maybe 15 minutes passed, people talking and snorting and smoking and answering phone calls. And Ancuta grabbed my hair, scaring me, jolting me out of my mad mindset as if I had been asleep. She pulled me upwards and I saw everyone was still in the room. The other girl was smoking again, looking my body up and down. Ancuta pushed me through the door into the dark corridor, past the exit door on the right, towards a room on the left.

There was a man there, just inside the door, waiting for me. Huge, maybe 55 years old. He reached out and helped her force me into the room.

And yes, it was a bedroom. Closed blinds, one lamp on in one corner. I stood at the side of the bed and he began taking off his clothes, his expression blank, maybe relaxed.

Ancuta slowly stepped back from the door, back into the corridor, staring at me.

And I said it.

'No.'

She stopped.

She marched forward, stamping on the ground, and I hid my face. She whacked me on the side of my head, on the back of my head. I felt a headache, a body ache, right as I stood there. She hit me again.

'Nooo!'

I screamed it.

The man reached to grab me. They both pushed me onto the bed and I hit his face. I scratched his skin. I was so strong in those moments. I felt like I could kill her and rip his face off at the same time.

But they pinned me, his hand round my neck, her hand slapping again and again at my head. I tried to pull away, onto my side to try to get myself to slip off the bed. And I felt her pressing my head down so hard into the sheets. I felt this woman then move onto me, climb onto me so she could sit on my head.

The man was pressing on my back, his hand on my lower back, pushing so hard I felt pressure all over and as if my spine would snap. He put a leg or an arm over my legs, I couldn't see, but it left me hardly able to move. I was jammed face down and deep into the mattress.

From there I did not move. At some stage Ancuta got off my head and left the room, but I do not remember when.

And now everything is unclear, the details of what happened and the things that I felt. But, yes, that was when I was raped for the first time in my life. I was raped from behind in a place I had never had or ever wanted to be used by a man.

It lasted maybe a minute, the noise of his hard breathing and panting, the quiet up and down noise of the bed. I wondered in one of those moments if he had used a condom, and it was maybe one of the most naïve things I have ever thought. Of course he did not use a condom. When he finished, he dressed and left. He did not say anything.

I know now that he is Albanian, a pimp and a pervert who has a reputation for helping to 'break in' girls, that he is one of the first impossible problems put in the way of new girls. He is a man who is a sex offender of the worst kind, because being a sex offender is his job.

After he walked out, I was alone for the first time since I had been walking down the street in London on that same day. I didn't now know the time, know what the weather was like, know if anyone in my house or at my work had asked where I was. I knew nothing, only that I had found myself in hell.

There were maybe just seconds before Ancuta was back in the room. She told me I was bleeding, to get off the bed. She grabbed at my arm and pulled me onto the floor. I went easy for her.

'Stand up,' she said, and slapped my head.

I did, as best as I could. I could feel the sticky blood. She took my arm and pulled me out of the room, my legs like jelly. Opposite was the door into the bathroom. The light was on. She pushed me into the shower cubicle,

'Clean yourself,' she said.

Chapter Eight

I knew nothing about Ireland. I knew it was a small country close to England, but it was not a place that featured in my life. I had seen some stupid horror movie about a little thing called a leprechaun with a suit and a beard, heard something about some violence there and I knew of a city called Dublin. I had no plan ever in my life to visit Ireland. But now my plans were no longer in my own hands.

My first day began in that bathroom. I washed myself in that shower, dried myself and sat down, sore, on the floor with the towel. I could not leave that room. I did not have the courage to open the door. I did not know what I would say, who I would see, what would happen. I did not know if that man was still there.

The day began with pain the way the night before had ended. But there was no dawn, no daylight, no new beginning to see. It was just a matter of sitting up, maybe waking up, cold, in that bathroom after maybe no sleep, maybe twenty minutes, maybe two hours, of sleep. I did not have any idea.

I had been taken only some number of hours before but already I had no idea what time it was. Maybe I was in shock. I don't know. Maybe my mind was so confused that it was telling me things that weren't true. I don't know. I don't know. I don't know. All I know is I was in that room for a while and a man came in to use the toilet. I had maybe been sleeping in there while others came and went, I don't know. But I watched as a man came in, a Romanian man I had not seen before, and he began to pee in the toilet. He said some words to himself, something quiet, and hardly looked at me. He walked out. He did not flush or wash his hands. Can you imagine I was thinking that when he left? I felt like saying, 'Flush the toilet, you pig,' but I didn't. That was the least of my problems. My freedom had been hijacked. My emotions were changing and falling apart. My principles were not important.

I have told you how I had heard the stories, the terrible stories, about what happens to some girls from Romania. But you should know I always thought girls in places like that were girls who had let themselves fall into a trap, girls who had not been as careful as I liked to think I was. I was never close to that world before, or at least I had never known that I had been close to that world. It would become clear that I had moved too close to it.

I looked at the taps on the sink for a while and was thinking how I was so thirsty, but I did not have the courage to touch them. Was this even a place with clean water? I didn't know. I knew nothing. I was half blind in what I could see and totally blind in what I knew.

I wrapped the towel around me and stood up. I could tell I was crying as I got to my feet and saw in the mirror. I was crying but my face and lips were so bruised and sore that I did not even know it. I pushed my hair back and pulled the towel around me, as if to make a dress.

So I took a deep breath and slowly opened the bathroom door. To the left was the open door to the living room, and I could see the back of a head and hear talking and phones ringing. To the right was one bedroom and in front of me was another bedroom.

The way out was on my left, just before the living room. The door was closed. If I opened it, there would be the steps down to the street and another external door below. It seemed as if it was 1,000 miles away but it was just there, just a few feet away from me. Would I be able to get to the door? Would it make a noise if I opened it? Would they catch me easily? What would they do? Would they kill me?

I walked towards it, shuffling a little bit as my body was not moving too well, and Vali turned his head to look from the living room.

'The blind one,' he said, and I froze.

Ancuta, wearing a blue robe, put her head around the door, blowing smoke, and stepped into the frame. The men continued chatting and she stayed still, looking into the dark corridor, glaring at me, first at the towel and then into my face.

The door to the other bedroom opened and I turned as a girl I had not seen before looked out. She waved a hand at me, as if to usher me towards the living room.

Ancuta beckoned me towards her. I walked slowly. She stepped out and grabbed my hair.

I screamed.

She pulled me into the living room and closed the door. She slapped me on one side of the head and then the other. There was no break in the conversation from the men. She slapped me again, my ears ringing, and pushed me back towards a wall.

'You don't shout in here, you blind bitch,' she said. 'No shouts or screams, blind bitch. Sit there,' she said, pointing at the sofa.

As I went to sit she grabbed the towel, pulled it away.

'Sit,' she said.

I counted three girls in that room, other than Ancuta, but I couldn't be sure. It was filled with smoke and my eyes hurt, my face hurt, and I didn't want to look around. I didn't know if making eye contact with someone would lead to my being hit again. I didn't know if keeping my head down and eyes on the floor would lead to my being hit again.

I didn't know if there was a possible friend in that room or if it was all just people who hated me.

There was a red rug on the floor, below the sofa, and I looked at my feet pressing into it. I thought how yesterday I would not have liked this cheap, dirty rug but that today I was seeing it as some kind of comfort.

A man came towards me and stood over me, smoking a cigarette. I looked up. He was drunk. It was Ilie Ionut, the one they called John. He lifted his hand and I cowered, just ducked down and hugged myself, waiting for it. When it didn't come I looked up. And then he hit me. His hand had been up all the time, waiting for me to look at him. He laughed a little bit, maybe enjoyed his little trick. He took another pull of his cigarette and walked back to his table, to his computer, to his phones.

One rang. A second one rang. One vibrated. All of them seemed to be active, or close to being active, all the time.

One tired girl, maybe 20, was getting a photograph taken in the corner. She was chewing gum, posing in lingerie on a chair, red satin pinned to the wall behind her. Carol was taking the pictures on a mobile phone. He said to her to pretend she had just heard a really good joke. The girl smiled.

Ancuta was with Bella, helping her to put on make-up and talking close together.

I could not know if these girls were paying off debts, if they were trafficked*, if they were volunteers, if they too had been stolen.

Ancuta said, 'So, blind one, would you like to have your picture taken?'

And it made her laugh. And when Bella saw her laugh, she laughed too. I didn't know if she was serious. A picture of my bruised and swollen face? To put on a website so they could advertise me for sex?

'No,' I said, my voice sore to use, my first word that morning, that day.

And she laughed again. The men laughed. The girls laughed. I put my head down.

I could see no food. There was no sign of anyone eating anything. I wanted food and I wanted water, but I was not brave enough, or stupid enough, to ask. So I stayed still and quiet, trying in some hopeless way to find out more about this situation, to blend in with the background in a room full of people.

The phones, always ringing, shaking, buzzing, and the door, always opening and closing. Girls – I think three in all – walked in and out, mostly not even looking at me. Sometimes they were naked, sometimes they were almost naked, sometimes in heels, sometimes not. Some of them took calls, some did not. They sat around as Ancuta flipped the catch on the exit door and let people in and out, but from where I was I could see no one.

The men worked on the laptops, chatted and drank and smoked and played poker and bingo online. And Ancuta came

* According to charity Stopthetraffik.org an estimated 21 million victims are trapped in modern-day slavery. Of these, some 4.5 million are sexually exploited.

and went, bossing around the room in her robe and talking about a holiday in Italy, about Madonna, about cigarettes and money and stupid girls.

When she came back into the room she would have money, euros, the kind of cash in use in the Republic of Ireland, the kind I had very rarely seen before. She would put it down close to Ilie. In a few moments he would pick it up, tuck it away. It was a busy, organised system.

I closed my eyes and thought I could try again to sleep, but she grabbed my hair.

'Do you want to know if your mother is okay?' she said.

'Yes,' I said. I had not thought of her safety in maybe half an hour. I must have been losing my mind.

Ancuta laughed. They all laughed.

'She is okay,' said Ancuta, 'she is still okay.'

There was never more than two or three minutes when she didn't look at me. They all kept looking at me, but she was watching me, always, always, always. I could feel it, my sore, cold skin crawling.

She kept going to Ilie, touching him, smiling at him, as if flirting with him. I would find out he was her partner, that they had a son back in Romania.

I sat there, starving, cold, thirsty, exhausted, for maybe hours. I'm guessing but it was probably around 6am or 7am when the girls were gone and there were only three of us left in the room. The girls had left to sleep in one bedroom and Carol had left to stay at whatever flats or other brothels he stayed at.

Ancuta, drunk and moody, had also left, glaring at me as she went, to sleep for a while with the girls, two or three phones in her hands.

Ilie and Vali sat at the table saying little, playing games, surfing the web. Ilie got up and boiled the kettle. He took out a pan and opened some beans up, poured them in. He put it on the hob. He took some bread from a cupboard and began to make toast. The smell was so strong, stronger than anything I knew.

He looked at me, maybe just once, as he was doing this, and I looked away.

Under his breath, just so I could barely hear it, he said, 'Don't fucking look at me, you bitch.'

I slept there, for a while, on the sofa. I didn't lie down, but pulled myself into a corner, arms wrapped tight around myself, and just switched off.

For how long, I don't know. What time was it when I woke? I don't know. From now on, for a long time, you must understand that they wanted me to lose track, to have to piece so many things together that I would have so few things to use like a foothold, to understand the day with, as they tried to derail my brain.

The phones in the living room – maybe 12 of them, maybe 20 – began to ring more and more and Ilie went to get Bella. She came, tired, exhausted, and sat there in lingerie, answering with a small, breathy voice. She got up and made herself a cup of coffee and smoked a cigarette. She didn't look at me at all.

When she had finished her cigarette, she poured a glass of tap water, and brought it to me. I looked and again thought, so totally crazily, if it was okay to drink the tap water in Ireland. But I would have drunk anything. Bella said nothing as I took it from her hand and drank. My lips were still sore. She had, I saw, bruises on her thighs.

'You can get a toothbrush in the bathroom cupboard,' she said, Romanian, from Bucharest, and she took the glass away again.

I didn't know if she meant for me to go and clean my teeth or not. I stayed where I was.

Another two girls came into the room and I wasn't sure if I had seen them before. They sat beside me but would not look at me.

Another pimp arrived and the men all stood to greet him, to shake his hand, to slap his shoulder, as if they had not seen him for a while. He was with two fully dressed girls, both looking very tired. They stood alongside him until he called for them to stand in the centre of the room, so Ilie could look at them. He checked them over then asked them to strip. They discussed how best to take photographs of them.

Ancuta returned in her robe, her hair freshly pulled back into a ponytail, perfume following her as she passed, ignoring me. The door began opening more and closing more, the phones starting ringing more and more pictures were taken of pouting girls in underwear in front of a red satin sheet pinned to the wall.

I just sat there.

Chapter Nine

Ancuta told me to get ready. She stood over me, looked at me like I disgusted her.

'Get ready, blind girl,' she said.

Maybe it was because I'd had a little sleep that I felt strong enough to say something to her.

'I want my clothes,' I said, and I knew she would react badly.

'You want your clothes?'

'Yes,' I said, feeling a glint of defiance rising up. 'And my glasses.'

'You want your clothes and your glasses?'

'Yes.'

There was a tiny moment where I really did think she was going to explain something, or tell me where they were, or say how I could get these things. Even though my first instinct told me she would be furious, it was a pause long enough to make me imagine there was some hope in all of this. And when that pause ended, so did the hope.

She pushed my face back with one hand and punched me in the side of the head. She punched and slapped and whacked at the side and back of my head again and again. I was screaming, my arms flailing out to reach at her, my eyes covered by the hand that was forcing my head back into the sofa.

'Fucking bitch,' she said, 'blind bitch, blind bitch.'

She was pulling my hair, gripping clumps of it and pulling it upwards again and again.

The men were laughing, whooping at the way she was attacking me with so much hatred, with so much frenzy.

I wanted to bite her, to get her hand or her face in my mouth and tear out lumps, but I was telling myself 'no, no, no' – some part of me was saying 'she will kill you if you do that'.

When she stopped I was deaf, my ears ringing, my face stinging, head stinging, my eyes crying, my whole body shaking.

She stood for a moment, then reached again for my hair, grabbing it and tugging me upwards to my feet. And you know I was taller than her, probably stronger than her, but she had all the cards, all the confidence, all the madness a person needs to be so controlling and cruel to another person.

I was dragged and shoved into the bathroom. She took a toothbrush from the cupboard, a used one, and told me to clean my teeth.

She took down a square bottle, some perfume of some kind, and sprayed it over my face as my shaking hand began to put paste on the toothbrush.

I kept my eyes closed and heard her leave the room. I brushed around my hungry mouth and spat it out into the sink, expecting to see blood and guts fall out of me, but there was none. But still I had the face of a beaten ghost.

Thirty seconds later she was back, holding lingerie, and handed it to me.

'Clothes,' she said, 'quickly.'

I put on the black thong and bra, both too small, both having been used by someone else. Maybe automatically, I pulled my hair back, as if to fix myself up.

Ancuta pulled her hand back as soon as I looked at her. I knew that if I had a knife I would stab her in the heart. I didn't flinch. For some reason I didn't move as that thought went through my mind.

She smiled, dropped her hand.

'There is someone to see you,' she said, and reached up to the cupboard.

She took out some lipstick.

The men were looking down from the living room as I stepped slowly out, a painted smile. Ancuta pushed open the door opposite and made space for me to walk in.

An old Irish man was leaning back on the bed, dangling his feet off the edge. He was maybe 60, 65.

'Hello, Natalia,' he said, looking at my body, staring openly and bluntly at my breasts and crotch. He stood up and winked at Ancuta behind me. I knew he must have known her from before. I thought not who he was, but who Natalia was. Was this what they were calling me?

'You look beautiful,' he said, looking right at my sore, red, slapped face. 'Come and sit on the bed, darling.'

He held his arm out as if to show me the way and I turned to see if she was there. She was just closing the door, nodding at me, advising me in her own sick way. I walked one step to the bed and sat down.

He stared at me, kept on staring as I sat there. I didn't know if I could or should speak. He wore shoes, a well-ironed shirt and old-man trousers. He had laid a blue jacket on the floor beside the bed. He bent down and grunted as he started untying his shoelaces.

'Lie back,' he said, taking them off.

He started to work on his buttons.

'Lie back,' he said, gesturing with his head.

I knew I would not, but I wasn't going to tell him anything.

'No?' he asked me.

I stayed still. He stepped closer, put his arms out as if he was going to take my shoulders, maybe to push me back.

And I snapped.

I slapped at his hands, at his half-open shirt. He stepped back and I stood up, started punching him in the stomach and face and throat.

He tried to drive me back, to grab hold of my arms, but I was moving too quickly, too crazy for him to catch me. I hit him again, hard on the nose, and he called, 'Anca! Anca!'

She was in right away, her boyfriend Ilie straight after her. They pulled me from the man and whacked me on the head. I was pushed onto the floor and slapped again and again on the back of the head and I screamed. I screamed like mad and like mad and like mad.

The man did not stay. He left with his shoes in his hands.

They dragged me to the living room and pushed me into a corner, onto the floor. Ancuta, or Anca, went to the kitchen area and returned with a knife. Black handle, a few inches long.

'I am going to kill your fucking mother in Sibiu,' she said.

'I can kill her by the telephone, just one call and some people will go up and stick a knife through her neck. They are always ready, the knife is always ready. Do you want that?'

I didn't speak.

'Do you want that, blind bitch?'

And again she slapped me. I was sure the blade would be stuck into my face. It was so close to me, jerking randomly in her angry hand.

'No,' I said. It was a stupid question.

'Do you want me to cut your tongue out and slash your face open right now?'

'No.'

'Do you want me to cut you up and feed you to pigs?'

'No.'

She slapped me on the back of the head.

'You fucking useless, stupid blonde bitch,' she said. 'You fucking blind, stinking bitch.'

More slaps, one for every word.

'You won't last any time without me here so you do what I say,' she said. 'I am keeping you alive, you blind cunt. You fucking cross me again and you will be cut into chunks of meat, you fucking bitch.'

She dragged me again to the bathroom, viciously stripped me and pushed my face against the wall. She pressed lipstick into my face, rubbed it all over my lips. It was everywhere, made me look like a clown, my swollen lips, my multicoloured freak-show face.

And she pushed me back into the corridor, one naked girl in heels standing out of our way, and back up to the living room.

She shoved me into that same corner and said, 'Stay ready, you blind whore. Always ready, you Sibiu bitch. You have work to do.'

I had known her only a few hours but I had seen her ten types of angry already. That one was the worst. There was sheer hate inside her for me, the sort of hatred that I was justified in having for her but not her for me. It was crazy. She was crazy.

She smoked a cigarette and pointed, told the men and girls what a bitch I was, that I didn't pay my debts and that people who don't pay debts get killed or worse.

I wanted to shout at her though a megaphone, 'What fucking debts, you nasty fucker?!' but I could not.

Had they got me mixed up with someone? Who did I owe money to? For what? When? How?

I was bursting with words and bursting with tears but I held all of it back as much as I could.

I can't remember if I was crying hard or not, but it didn't really matter. It would have made no difference to me or anyone else. I was so hungry and thirsty and weak and wanted to die so much that nothing at all really mattered anymore. And the phones were ringing and buzzing all the time.

Between her fits of flirting and slapping and shouting she answered some, dropping into a low, calm voice, and arranging times and talking sex and cash and fun and how nice it was for some guy to phone. This place was an asylum run by the lunatics.

It was 100 euros here, 80 euros there, 160 euros here, 200 there. 'Baby' here, 'Yes baby' there, 'No baby' here. In-calls, out-calls, one girl, two girls.

And always she kept watching me, looking at me after every sentence, looking at me when she answered and ended every call.

Ilie was at a laptop, a new bottle of whisky on the table beside him. He and another pimp, also Romanian, were drinking, two short glasses.

He turned to me, smiled, said, 'I think you maybe want some whisky, blind one? You're full of high spirits and energy, maybe you need a drink?'

I shook my head. I didn't.

He lifted his glass, held it out to me.

'Drink some,' he said, 'it helps.'

'No,' I said, 'thank you.'

And Ancuta came close, watching this, looking at me with that rage and hate in her eyes.

'She doesn't deserve whisky,' she said, 'not one drop.'

Ilie shrugged and took the glass away. He kept looking at me and downed it.

'It's good,' he said. 'Irish whisky. The only good thing in this country.'

The other man laughed.

Ancuta stared.

Ilie said, 'We will be getting some food later and, if you want to have some, you have to make sure I want to give you some, you understand? Like the other girls, okay? They don't shout or fight and they eat and sleep. Do you understand that, blind one?'

I didn't move, didn't speak.

'I know you understand,' he said. 'You're a smart woman and you understand.'

Ancuta was answering calls, still glaring at me.

I did not know if I should shake my head or nod my head. I did neither.

Ancuta said quietly, a little while later, 'I have people for you to meet. They will be here soon. Get ready.'

There were to be two of them. They were two young men who had been out drinking for the afternoon, who decided they wanted a girl to share, a girl who would do everything and anything.

Both had spoken with Ancuta before. She told me as she passed me the black lingerie again, straightened up the lipstick and applied the eye pencil to my face, that they had been open with her about their needs.

'They want a blonde,' she said. 'And if you hit them, they will hit you back.'

They met Ancuta before she opened the door and brought me to them. I was sitting on the bed, my heart pounding.

They looked at me, not as if they were going to tell me I was beautiful, but as if they didn't like me at all.

Ancuta nodded towards me, catching my eye as she closed the door. I had a feeling she would have stayed to watch if she could have done so.

The men stood there. One took off his jacket, rubbed his face.

'You been a hooker for long?' the other one said, his words slurred from drinking.

'I am not a hooker,' I said, my voice as small and as pathetic as I looked.

'Serious?' he said. 'I just paid for you!'

The other man said, 'Maybe she does it for fun.'

'That's it.' The other man laughed. 'A slut.'

I was so uncomfortable, I cannot tell you.

The other one took his jacket off. He came round the back of the bed and the other one came towards me. I felt hands on my shoulders from behind. The other one reached out for my thighs, as if to spread them.

I tried. I did try. I really was thinking that I could do this and get it done and get back to working out whatever it was I was trying to work out.

I tried but I could not stand it.

My hand flew up and whipped into the face in front of me. The guy gave a sort of a scream and pulled away, in total shock. The one behind started forcing me downwards, as if to lay me down, and my hands started slapping everywhere. I was shouting and punching at 1,000mph and he backed off. Both of them backed off quickly. They looked at each other, picked up their coats and left the room. But I had won nothing. I had only made things worse.

Chapter Ten

When the doors were closed, there were customers there. When the doors were open, there were none.

Often both bedroom doors were closed. Men would arrive at the top of the stairs, meet Ancuta and she would take them to the room where the girl was waiting.

The living-room door would, most of the time, stay closed. The chatting in there would be quiet. Men do not want to hear men's voices, to see other men, when they arrive to have sex with a woman in an illegal place.

Ancuta, the Mother Pimp, would not let customers see each other. The girl would leave the room first and check it was okay to let the man out. He would then scurry out, as they all do, maybe giving her a ridiculous goodbye kiss. She would open the exit door and he would rush down the stairs by himself and out onto the street.

It was almost constant. Morning, when men were going to work or taking a mid-morning break, was popular. Then lunchtime, also busy, some arriving with a plastic bag holding their sandwiches and crisps, ready to eat after they screwed. It was steady through the afternoon, then busy again at dinnertime. And from around 8pm, it was busy all night. At the weekends in a city like Galway, the men could be arriving at one o'clock or two o'clock or four o'clock in the morning. Pimps do not like to refuse business. The men would always be drunk at that time. The buzzer would go at the front door and, by the time the man had made it to the top of the stairs, Ancuta would know how drunk he was.

The rules were that most things were on the menu, as long as the girls were not damaged by the men, or in any way made so that they could not work anymore. The only people who could really leave bruises on us were our pimps, and mostly Ancuta.

She was so nice to the customers, but she hated them all too. They were bastards, she would say.

She would call them stupid and ugly and dirty and stinkers behind their backs. But when they showed up at her door, she would wink and smile and show them to where they could do what they liked to a young stranger.

And sometimes she would take them too. Her body was, like all the other female bodies in the range of Ilie and his friends, advertised online and sometimes the men would request her.

When she didn't want it that way, she was in the position where she could pass them on to someone else. When she was okay with it, she would do it with them. She was a career prostitute, one who had been recruited as a street girl in Bucharest by Ilie and who ended up as one of his girls in Ireland and eventually as his own Mother Pimp in Galway. She had been brainwashed by being starved of control, then given some control, some power, some status, and she loved herself so much because of that it was obscene.

After the time I frightened off two drunk Irishmen, she said I had made life very difficult for my mother back home. In a way I didn't care because I wasn't sure they would do anything to her. How would I even know if they could, if they would, if they did? I had no contact with the outside world so they could so easily just tell me lies and I had no way of checking.

And part of me also thought that whatever might happen to my mother could not be worse than what was happening to me. Death is not worse than that.

Ancuta sent me to the living room and I sat on a chair, naked, starving, staring with my bleary eyes at the blinds covering the windows that looked out to the street. There was covering on the windows too, some material taped to the glass to black out the day and the night, but I could not be sure what it was.

I found a corner, at the top, on the right, where there seemed to be a patch of naked glass, a piece of glass that would allow me to tell if it was day or night, a piece out into the world. I found myself staring at this little square of glass and thinking how all I needed in the world was through there. And I looked hard at it and thought of my mother and my grandmother. For maybe the first time after diving into my memories, I realised I was not crying, not going to cry.

Ilie was watching. He had returned from playing poker nearby, which was something he liked to do. He would often disappear and reappear an hour or five hours later. He had his own place and ran other girls in the city, usually girls who were staying with other pimps, and, as the big boss, was always checking on how his business was going.

I wondered if pimps were always on the street outside, watching the door, watching the customers who came and went, checking that the police did not arrive. Maybe they were always in contact with the people inside from the outside, telling them everything that was going on.

Later on Ancuta put me in the bedroom where some of the girls were sleeping. She told me to lie on the floor. I did and felt myself curling up into what they say is the foetal position. I was starving, cold all the time, and felt I would faint at any moment.

After a while she returned, opened the door to the room, staggering drunk, and stood over me, wearing jeans and a T-shirt.

'Are you sleeping, blind one?' she said.

Her tone was almost tender. I did not know what to do.

'Are you awake, blind one?'

I was wide awake, lying still.

She put her hand down, gently took a good grip of my hair and then pulled hard. I screamed and she was still pulling. I tried to get her hands off me but she was winning, pulling my head, face down, to the place just where she wanted it. I saw her feet as she moved. And the door slammed on my head.

It was a full and complete sensation of pain, of head and jaw and teeth being hammered at the same time. She did it again, as I was pulling back, and I did not get away in time.

I pulled back again and curled up, feeling like my whole face and ears and head were cracked open. She slapped my breasts, my stomach, my arms, and started ranting and raving and insulting me non-stop. Other girls were lying awake and still as this was happening, as a fellow young woman from Romania was doing this to another young woman from Romania. But I do not blame them for saying or doing nothing. What could they have done?

I knew, of course, Ancuta would not stop. There was no way this woman would be swayed from her duties. She was cruel and evil to the fingernails, from under the fingernails to the inside of her bones. The blood in my mouth I could taste then, from my gums, my teeth, was a strong signal that she was going to destroy me.

I was brought to the other bedroom later and given no lingerie. She sprayed perfume on me as I sat there like a shell, my head feeling like it was being crushed. She told me to smile, slapped my face and told me to smile, and I smiled as the next man came into the room. He knew her as well. He had called her Anca outside, after he spoke with her, paid her and came in to see the difficult new girl. Lots of the men love the new girls, difficult or not.

This one joked that because I was naked I was ready for him already. He told me that I was pretty and my breasts were nice and they would fit his hands very well, as if this was meant to be.

I resisted him, not with my fists, but with my body. I had no choice. I was frozen up, my muscles were trying to forbid him to enter me as he lay on top, his stubble and hairy chest rubbing all over me. But he didn't mind that at all. He liked it.

He asked me if I had any condoms and I didn't respond. They were in a drawer beside the bed, but he was just maybe going through the motions. At that stage if I had a disease that was going to kill me, I would have been glad of it.

The man felt me up and raped me in the way he wanted and was gone in five minutes. He kissed me on the forehead, his sweaty face pressing on my skin, as he finished putting his belt on.

'Thank you,' he said and walked out of the room.

I lay there, my kidneys hurting, my stomach sore inside, and I felt around my dirtied mouth with my tongue. A tooth at the back was loose, maybe cracked, and I didn't know if it was sore or not. There was the taste of blood again. Blood and semen. I wanted to be sick.

Ancuta came in, looked at me. She told me to clean up any mess and get out quick. She told me to get into the shower, to get washed down. It must all be done quick, she said. In the bathroom I found she had put some bleach in a soap dish instead of soap. She told me later that it was the best way to kill the germs, that it was only for me because I was so special.

'Be quick,' she said after I washed, 'we are busy.'

In the living room they were ordering food and I don't even remember wanting any. Ilie kneeled in front of me as I sat on the sofa. He said he did not have a television because he thought it was bad when it came to people concentrating on business. I didn't look at him. He gave me a bag of McDonald's chips.

'Hungry?' he said.

'No,' I said.

'Stubborn woman,' he said. 'You should wear more make-up.'

I didn't reply.

'I hope you wash better next time,' he said. 'You stink of cum.'

We slept when we could, but with the bedroom doors open. In general, they didn't like us to sleep. The pimps came and went and there were always at least one or two there – Vali, Ilie, Carol – working in some kind of shift pattern. Ancuta would rarely go out but when she did she liked to walk around the nice shops and buy nice things and look in the windows of travel agents at trips to Italy.

For me it seemed as if the normal things were now not normal. It was not sensible for my body to tell me I was hungry, thirsty, cold. It was not a good idea to try to sleep or I would have someone coming to check if my eyes were closed and to hit me if they were. There was no pattern or sense or routine. Girls came and went and I could not always be sure of faces, if I had seen this one or that before, and it wasn't helped by the fact that my vision was so poor. The thin girl I knew as Bella – the first girl I saw at that flat – was one who went away, never to be seen again, never to be spoken of again. It seemed to me as if she was replaced with another girl, because it was not long after she had gone that another frail little girl arrived with a pimp, a timid little blonde they called Skinny, 18 years old. From this time on, as with me, Skinny would always be in that flat.

Sometimes one or two of the girls would chat, but it seemed for days as if they had been told not to speak with me, as if I was vermin to be avoided. I wanted to know what their situations were, but it would be a while before I could find out any real truths about anything that was going on.

Ancuta and Ilie had somewhere else, somewhere she would keep all the things she liked to say she had bought. She would eat and sleep in the living room, sleep in the bedrooms when it was quiet, but she never, ever wanted to miss a single customer. This was like her drug. I thought how she must be making so much money and saving it up for something. No one could do what she did for too long. Even if you were a twisted bitch, it would wear you out. But she was giving almost everything to Ilie.

At busy periods, everyone was in the living room, smoking and drinking and going quiet when someone was answering a phone.

The girls were advertised on the perfectly legal Escort Ireland* website, the biggest sex-for-sale site in the country,

* According to filed accounts, Escort Ireland turned over €6,026,465 (around £5.3m) in 2015. It was co-founded in 1998 by Peter McCormick, a former police officer from Belfast, Northern Ireland.

which is paid to host images and details about girls. There were pictures of them, smiling in their lingerie, blowing kisses to the camera, in places that looked so warm and inviting.

The men would edit the pictures for a long time, boosting colour and adding atmosphere, before posting them up. They would make up names, laugh about it when they were filling in the bios, advise customers about ages and nationalities they were making up on the spot. They would work out values, who was worth what, who would work best where, and list how much the girl would cost for whatever amount of time.

There is a ratings system on the website, where men can tell other men what they thought of their time with the girl, if she looks like her pictures, if she smiled and chatted, if she refused to do anything or if she just let them do what they want, even what they thought of where she is based, of the privacy, if they felt as if they might be seen, if they felt uneasy because they saw any other men around.

They comb through the pictures and find the girl they want to have sex with, look at her bust size, at all those reviews, check her height and willingness to do certain things, and have a look at the price.

Then they call a number, a certain number in use for a time for that girl, and maybe Ancuta or Skinny or one of the girls who had been brought to the brothel by another pimp would answer.

They will have a short discussion, he will say if he wants 30 or 60 minutes, and then he will be told which street he should come to in Galway and a time will be fixed. When the man arrives, he rings again to say he is on the street and he is given the exact address. A buzzer goes a few minutes later and he is let inside. He comes up the stairs and meets either Ancuta or one of the girls and she takes him to the room. The money is paid up front and taken from the room by, or to, Ancuta.

It is never 30 minutes. It is never 60 minutes. The man thinks he will fill his time by making her fall in love with him, or he will make her do wonderful foreplay and they will both have a lovely time. But when the door closes and he is in the room with a near-naked girl with a tired face and bruises on her legs, when he has no idea what sort of, if any, men might be sitting in the other room, when it becomes real that he is breaking the law and that being found here could destroy not just his own life but also his family's, he does not want to stay around for very long. He knows we are all part of a secret, criminal world and he does not want to be in that world longer than he has to be.

He gets excited, touches himself, slaps, insults, abuses, pours love in an ear, gets slapped, or goes to the toilet or whatever it is, and then he leaves. He wants a good cum and, if it takes five minutes or ten minutes or twelve minutes, most of the time it does not make any difference. When he is done, he goes.

And you know, I keep calling them 'men'. I keep saying to you that these people are men. They are not, to me, men. They are not good men. They are wrong men, stupid men, selfish men, and I hate them all. So very many of them to hate, but I promise you I hate them all. I cannot feel any other way about these sorts of people. I hate all the men who raped me and who raped all the other girls. I have to. It would be wrong not to hate such men.

So for our purposes, from now on I will not call them men. I will not call them customers or clients or any other bullshit name. I will call them assholes. That is the name for the men who raped me from this point onwards – assholes.

Ilie again wanted me to drink whisky when he saw my teeth were bleeding. Ancuta told me to drink some too, saying that it was a disinfectant. She said she didn't want my mouth to stink of illness.

She put some white bread and butter on a plate and gave it to me. She said I should eat this and clean my mouth out with the whisky afterwards.

I nodded. It was her most sensitive act to date. I ate some pieces of bread, not too much, and then sloshed some whisky around and swallowed it. It was horrible. I don't like whisky. I thought I would not drink the stuff again.

She gave me the black lingerie and said to look after it. It didn't fit me properly, it had already been someone else's, but now it was mine. It was maybe the only thing I owned.

'Wash it in the kitchen,' she said, 'not in the machine.'

I said, 'Okay.'

'I can maybe get you a robe too, you know? Just maybe, you know?'

I nodded.

Chapter Eleven

Days passed.

I wondered what had happened with my room in north London. Was Marco still there? Was he paying my rent? What about my things? My laptop, clothes, my pieces of jewellery had all been left behind. Would he have heard anything about what might have happened?

And my mother, what might she be thinking? Did she think I had cut her out of my life in the way that she had cut me out of hers at Christmas? My phone would not be answered anymore, my text messages probably unread.

Even my job – the people I worked for. I had bookings, I had keys, and I had just vanished without saying a word to anyone. Would they call the police?

My friends on Facebook, would they be wondering? I did not say much on Facebook but surely someone would see if they could message me sooner or later?

Ilie had asked me for my email and Facebook passwords and I had told him I would not give them to him. I didn't know why he wanted them, but I said I would not be helping him.

He thought that was so funny.

'It doesn't matter, blind girl,' he said in his Roma dialect, looking me up and down as if he knew something I did not know.

He had pictures taken of me, even though I had bruises, even though I looked like hell, even though I did not pose properly. They were naked pictures, pictures of me in lingerie. He took them and I did not care.

In time, I would find out what he did with them. They were put on Facebook, from my own account, with a message from 'me' telling my friends I had found a new life as an illegal prostitute in a secret place. In this message I was bragging that I was rich.

Carol's plan was to go back to London. He stayed for a few weeks, meeting up with pimps he knew in the city and in Dublin. A lot of the prostitution in Ireland is controlled from Dublin, a lot of the pimps building their horrible little empires there with trafficked girls before moving them around the country and into Britain and elsewhere.

It became clear that Ilie had some problems with people he had known from before in Dublin and I learned that he ran his own show in Galway, that he had defied big pimps in Dublin in the past.

For Carol it was different; he was the small fish who kept a few friends everywhere but was not very important. When he was going back to London, he fixed a price for me. His job was done. I had been accepted. He had sold his product, his stolen goods. He wanted 30,000 euros for me and would return to Crina in London with the money. Who knows, between them they might maybe find, through friends of friends of friends, another girl who fitted their plans. Ilie gave him the money in cash.

The sum of 30,000 euros is higher than most girls are traded for, but it is not too high. The account had been reset for my new owner, Ilie, and now it was me, and also Skinny, who he owned outright in that little flat above the bookies. They were clear and open about my value; it was no secret. And Ilie was clear when he said I would not now be worth anything until I had made him 30,000 euros.

Maybe in your head you are thinking now that I was about to start thinking in a different way than I had been before? Maybe because I still clenched my fists but did not, on every occasion, throw them at assholes, you think, 'Ah yes, Anna is now working properly for the pimps. She is the blind one who is going to earn Ilie 30,000 euros now.'

If you think it was as simple as that, you are wrong.

Let me explain this to you – I have hit many men, many assholes. I have hit hundreds of assholes.

I have punched them in the face and the balls. I have scratched and slapped them. I have refused and resisted and been successful. And I have refused and not been successful.

Many assholes liked it when I fought back, and that made things worse for me. Many hated it and ran away in terror and that made things worse for me. Many times I resisted only with the inside of my body, and that made me hurt like hell again and again and again. But, you know, the pimps will always hit you anyway, they will always slap and beat you for some reason, they will always have a point to make. I saw Ancuta hit all the girls who visited that place, although she hit none of them as much as she hit me.

When a bad review was left, one that said, 'Oh this girl refused this or this girl was in a bad mood', that would make her really angry. Bad reviews were bad for business, she said. But most assholes do not leave any reviews, good or bad, so there were times when I pushed them away from me and they left and never complained. But there were times too when they complained to Ancuta that I would not do what I was told. Yes, some of them would go crying to Mama when they could not make me do what they wanted. These must be the most pathetic people in the world.

Sex without condom? No. I said no. Every time. They would whine to me that they had paid for sex without condom and I would say, 'I don't care.' They would say, 'Why?' and I would say quietly, 'I have AIDS.'

And then they would shit themselves, they would understand.

Up the ass? No. I said no. Every time. Why not?

I would say, 'Because it is my ass so you are just going to have to live with your problem, we all have problems. Complain if you want. I don't care.'

They might say, 'I'm going to ask for my money back,' and I would say, 'Fine, go and ask those guys in the living room for your money back,' and they would never do that. No pimp will ever give money back to anyone.

But some assholes don't just not care about you, they like it more when things go bad for you. They like to really get into the idea of rape, they like to hurt, to insult and abuse. They want you to be unhappy, to see you bleed or cry and witness the hopeless rage inside of you.

And when I hit assholes like that, they always hit back. They would squeeze and twist my breasts, my vagina, punch my stomach, grip my throat to the point that they were holding my life in their hands. They would do that with hard-ons, happy to be rubbing themselves and beating this hungry, unhappy girl from Romania.

None of them wants to hear about you. Many of them want you to have some conversation with them, but they want it to be simple, convenient, maybe happy or sexy. Some of them love to hear a sad, bad story. I knew the truth of what happened to me would excite some sadistic assholes, but I never told them. I never told anyone the full truth. Not at first, not for a while.

In the first week or two weeks one asshole wanted to kiss some boots of a particular size and asked Ancuta if she could find that girl. She told me to go in the room and wait for a man with boots. I sat on the bed and he came in, a man in his thirties, Irish, nervous and polite.

He put them on me and told me not to do anything, to sit there and wait and he would not take long. He took all of his clothes off and kissed them, the long black leather boots, from one end to the other and masturbated. When he came, he did it in his own hand and kept on kissing as it happened. Then he asked me to take off the boots as he got dressed. This sort of asshole was the best kind of person, the highest-quality person, I would meet.

Girls who were being sold in Galway often came to the flat to get their picture taken there because it was a place known by a lot of pimps. Romanian, Albanian, Hungarian, whatever, many of them went through that shit-hole flat, many of them trying to keep their contact up with Ilie.

If you ask me how much business was going on there in those two bedrooms, I would tell you I don't know. But I can tell you the things I do know. I can say that if this business interests you, maybe disturbs you and maybe you have read things about it before, you will have read that such and such a girl was 'seeing 10 men a day' or 'seeing 15 men a day.' Maybe that is how you make sense of the business and how much money can be made. But that is nonsense. Those figures are stupid. They are an easy way to make people who live in a normal world work out what is going on. It is often the girls themselves who say that, who try to paint a clearer picture.

Let me tell you that many of the girls trafficked into prostitution have no idea how many assholes they see. They see the assholes when the assholes want to be seen. So many girls will not know when the day ends and begins. They will not know what any average is because they are being used over and over again without a break. There is nothing average about being raped again and again, all day, every day. When everything blends into everything else, when the long, hungry days don't end or begin, there is no brain in the world that can draw up a graph of what has happened.

But if you want me to help you understand this, I will take you back to the 30,000 euros. That is what changed hands for me. It was the value someone placed on me. Once they felt I was ready to see more assholes, once they felt I had been worn down and was hungry and tired and lost enough to not punch every asshole they sent to see me, they started counting.

It took 13 days. In 13 days I made them 30,000 euros. For every 30-minute booking they took 80 or 100 euros, depending on the advertisement. For every 60-minute booking they took as much as 160 or 200 euros.

Thirteen days.

You work it out.

Some of the girls wanted to be like Ancuta. She had been a prostitute in Bucharest, where the pimps stick the girls on the street and work them hard, where they tell them they can send them to London or Paris or Stockholm to have a lovely time.

Ancuta came from that background but saw a way through it, had her brain broken so much that she saw a future in accepting it and working with the pimps as a Mother Pimp, which is what all brothels want – a woman to manage women.

She worked for Ilie in London for a while and ended up with him in Galway. That city is a busy place in Ireland for prostitutes, with many brothels, and many asshole visitors know they will be able to get what they want there.

Being the Mother Pimp in Galway was for Ancuta a big step up, a place to work where there would be many, many clients, all arriving as tourists – Irish or English or American or anything else – and many festivals and horse races and concerts in the pretty old city beside the sea.

All she needed to be a Mother Pimp, to be responsible for making many thousands of euros every week, was to be an insane bitch from hell and to not care one bit about anyone but herself.

She worked many hours, hating and forcing and tricking and stealing and bringing in all the cash. In her own way she was house-proud, always cleaning the floor, mopping the hall, bedrooms and bathrooms, when there was space between assholes. She wanted me to do it too, wanted all the girls to be quick to get the mop or the brush when they could, but I think she liked most doing it herself because maybe it gave her some sort of ownership of the terrible place.

Ancuta, Anca or Cami to those who knew her best, talked a lot about Italy. It was a place that seemed to appeal to her because she believed Italian women looked fantastic, dark and confident and beautiful, and that is how she liked to see herself. She was a woman of no depth and who I think was in truth more blind than me.

She would keep herself tanned, with her nails manicured, and liked to wear branded clothing. She would disappear for two hours or so and come back saying how her friends in the shops thought this hat looked so nice on her, or how this make-up was the best that a person could buy in the city, that it was used on catwalks in Milan.

Did she ever think, when she was announcing this all around the living room, that she was saying things that just proved she was even more stupid and hateful? I do not think so.

Her arrangement was to manage the girls who were in that flat when they came to work. It might be for a day or a few days and then they would move back to their previous pimp or on to another pimp. She was not really a pimp herself, just the woman who had been taken apart so well that she thought she was in a good job. The men were the pimps, deciding on the girls, sorting out the deals, protecting the business and setting up the profiles online.

Some of the girls would talk to Ancuta about her nails, about her business, about helping them maybe get into the business end of things, and she would speak to them like she was some kind of genius. I think they all hated her, but they knew that to be on her right side was better than being on her wrong side.

Yet even though she might be friendly at times with one or two of the girls, she would hit them all. Her little hands were hard from slapping faces and, most of all, backs of heads. She had to remember not, as Ilie reminded her many times, to mark faces.

She gave him the cash, or some of the cash, and he would roll it up and pocket it. He would take the cash away and wire it to his people in Romania and keep a lot of it too.

He drove a BMW car and always stank of cologne. He wore stupid branded tracksuits and typed lies with fingers wearing gold rings on stolen laptops. He went driving now and then, sometimes running a trusted girl to somewhere for an out-call, or sometimes dropping off cash or picking up food.

I was never spoken to in the way the other girls were. I did not become one of the girls who wanted to be like Ancuta.

That is why it was weeks and weeks before they took my picture for the website. They could not be sure that I was on board with their criminal operation and did not, I assume, want to put evidence of me onto the internet. They used other pictures to advertise me, pictures of another blonde girl with her head turned away from the camera. They said I was Natalia, Lara, Rachel, whatever, and that I was 18 or 19 or 20 or 21 and that I was Latvian, Polish, Czech, Hungarian. It didn't matter. None of that stuff matters.

They had other pictures of me too, the ones they had put on my Facebook page. And, you know, they had made sure they had been reported. And, you know, Facebook had closed down my page. I had, they said, posted sexual images.

It was only a few weeks after I was taken from the street that I was gone from social media.

Chapter Twelve

Ancuta woke me up on the floor in a bedroom. I had nothing over me as other girls were sleeping in the bed.

She pushed me on the shoulder with her toe, said, 'Anna, get up, quickly.'

She grabbed my face as I stood up fast. She told me to get wide awake.

'A man wants to see you,' she said, pushing me into the bathroom.

I cleaned my teeth and she told me to put on make-up and make sure there was no vaginal hair.

'Cream and razor,' she would say all the time, 'cream and razor the mess.'

She inspected me, looked me all over. I remember it was the first time I asked her a hard question.

'Can I talk to my mother?'

I thought it was better than saying, 'How long are you keeping me for?'

Or better than, 'Will you let me go?'

She was surprised.

'You have been drinking too much whisky,' she said. 'Your mother is okay.'

I said I had been drinking, but often I had been spitting it out, only trying to numb the pain of my teeth. They had been cracked at the back, damaged by the slamming of the door on my head.

Maybe I was drinking too much of that horrible whisky. I don't know. I didn't know. I have no clear chart for you, no way to explain what was happening to me, what I or anyone else was doing to my body.

'We can talk after,' she said. 'This man wants time with you.'

She rushed me into the room and I sat. There was an overhead light with no bulb, and one lamp with a dark-blue shade on the bedside cabinet. The window, as always in the bedrooms, was closed with the blinds down and curtains pulled. It was dark, but everywhere was dark except the living room. Although my eyesight was so bad I never really saw the detail of what was going on in there anyway.

Ancuta opened the door and a man in a suit and a long winter coat came in. She nodded at me as she closed the door. He was maybe 50, holding a bottle of wine and two glasses. He looked drunk. In fact he looked sad. There was no smile. He sat on the bed and sighed. I wondered if he had walked down the street and in through the door with the wine and glasses, or had Ancuta given them to him?

'Hello,' he said.

I nodded.

'Do you want a drink?'

I shrugged. I didn't care. He unscrewed it and poured the glasses.

We sat in silence.

'I want to ask you something,' he said.

There had been a girl he met in Dublin, a girl in a brothel, and he had got to know her well. He told me who she was. Did I know her? I told him no. I said I didn't know many people. He said he had seen her many times, that they had become close. He took her out for dinner, she stayed with him overnight in hotels. They had been to the cinema, he said.

I was thinking, 'So what, asshole? I don't care about you or this girl.'

He said she had worked with Ancuta in Dublin and now he had learned Ancuta was in Galway.

'Ancuta does not recognise me,' he said. 'I am asking you in secret, discreetly, if you know who that girl is, the one I am talking about?'

I said I did not.

'If you ever see this girl,' he said, 'I would really like to know.'

This all meant nothing to me.

I said, 'I don't know people. I am not here by choice.'

And then, as I sometimes did, I said, 'My English not good.'

He nodded. 'I understand. It must be so difficult here with the language and everything else.'

I agreed.

And we sat with our wine, him in his suit, me in the underwear.

He told me he had loved her, or thought he had loved her.

'She was bringing her family over from Romania,' he said. 'And I paid for it.'

And this was what he was wanting to tell me. He said he had given thousands of pounds to this girl, helping her, buying her things, giving her money to send to her family to buy plane tickets. He said it was like she had taken him for a fool every time they met and that she had cost him a lot. But now she was gone, he said.

'I can't help,' I said. 'Ask Ancuta.'

'Okay,' he said. 'It's just you're new here and I thought you might know something about her. I don't think Ancuta would be helpful, do you?'

'No,' I said.

He told me he did not want to have sex.

This asshole worked for a big computer firm and seemed rich. But he was hurt and angry. In my mind he was the first and last cause of his own problems, but then he wasn't interested in anything I could tell him.

Do you know I could have told him I was trafficked and he would have nodded and drunk from his glass? Do you know I could have said I was taken from a street and put in this hole and that my world had been shrunk to a few rooms filled with sweating half-naked men and I had not seen the sun for I don't know how long? He would have agreed with me that this was not nice.

That is the level of humanity I was dealing with. Level zero. People do not want to know. They either want sex, want some sort of assistance or they do not want to know you. And when they have had sex, they do not want to know you.

That asshole came to see me three times, always drunk and always to just sit on the bed and tell me that someone had taken some of his money under false pretences. I felt like strangling him.

What a fool.

But they are all fools. It takes for you to lose your freedom to realise just what fools free people can be.

Most of them were aged maybe 35 to 55 and I think most of them were not happy people. They feel they have so much responsibility for things, or their job is too hard, or they owe too much money, and coming to see a fantasy girl lets them forget it all.

For them it's like taking a bag of drugs – they are driven to it, it makes them feel good and then they use it up and throw the bag away.

I had become a disposable product, like some backstreet drug. I was cheap to own and I made lots of money. I was a brand, a type, and the girls are always types. The assholes want black hair or blonde hair or red hair, always some kind of preference. She has to be skinny or tall or busty or petite or whatever, and most of the time she has to be young as they can get. But none of those things are types of people, you understand? They are all fantasy types but in the real world there is no such thing as a fantasy girl, it is just a girl who has ended up somehow being the human form of a picture in somebody's mind.

I had so many names that I can't even tell you. I was told I was one name by Ancuta sometimes, and then sometimes told by the customers that I was someone else from somewhere else.

And I was told to speak very little, to not get into conversations with the assholes because it wastes time and they don't want you to know anything, and they don't want to know anything about you. Ancuta said she often listened to conversations, if they took place, and I don't know if that was true.

I think maybe her conversations with the customers were of more interest than mine. She sent one asshole to me who wanted me to shit on him. Another girl had refused to be with him and Ancuta said I would have to do this.

When he arrived he looked just like a normal man, but it was his deepest desire to have a girl poo into his mouth. He wanted to lie on the floor and for me to stand over him, then to come down low to make sure it got into his face and he was able to eat it.

I sat in the room with him and told him I was not ready, and I knew that I would never be ready. He said he didn't mind and would wait as long as it would take.

After his time was up Ancuta came to the door and asked if it was okay. I said I couldn't help this man. He said he would wait as long as it took, hours if needed. But he had to go then, Ancuta told him, because the room was needed. He would have to book a longer time.

I hoped I would never see him again. I hoped I would never see any of the assholes again. I hoped they would all go and fall off cliffs or crash their cars or get crushed under rocks or catch diseases that would make their arms and legs and penises fall off.

But my problem was that I was making the money they wanted me to make. Assholes liked to be with me, they liked my body, my attitude. It must have been obvious that I did not like them, that I could not really see them properly. It must have been clear to them that I was not jolly, that I was hungry and bruised. They must have known I was trafficked because that was clear in every word I said, every move I made, the constant marks on my neck, my legs and arms.

After Carol left and I made them so much money in so few days, Ancuta told Vali and Ilie I was their 'million-dollar baby'. She said it was funny because I was blind and had been so angry, but here I was being their moneymaker.

And her million-dollar baby was eating the last parts of a carton of Chinese takeaway with cracked back teeth. She was looking at bones and rice, drinking a glass of water with no clothes on. This million-dollar girl had skin sores from washing so much, sometimes with bleach, to get the filth off her body. She had aching insides and constantly sore knees and thighs. She looked like death and she was losing her mind.

The pimps in Galway knew my reviews were leading to more and more people coming to see me, that I was the girl of the moment, or at least one of them, in the city. All of that meant I was sellable, that I had a good value, and that was why the pimps were interested.

Do you know that some of the girls who passed through there hated me because of that? That's how strange this world is. It was popular to rape me, to use me all day and night like a battery hen for sex, and they thought I was having a more successful life than them.

I remember trying to work it out, wondering at what point I might jump up and say to Skinny, to some of the others coming to that place, that they had no value in that place, that the more they made the less they were worth, not more.

But these are the things you think about, but never do, when you are held somewhere, when you are stuck in a place in the world like time has frozen. This is the crap that goes through a hopeless mind.

These things would get thought often when I sat in that one place on the sofa, staring at the top right-hand corner of the window at the little piece of glass, the little patch that showed if it was night or day or somewhere in the middle.

I was always trying to work out what time it was, always unable to read the assholes' watches and never wanting to ask them. It was no secret, it did not matter to anyone if I knew what time it was, but I felt as if giving up on knowing the time was like giving in yet more, surrendering more.

I would sit on that seat and think I might soon be killed by someone, or be killed by my own hand. I would think how my body would never be presented to any official and that my mother, my friends back in Romania, would never know what had become of Anna.

Chapter Thirteen

The first time I left that place was in June. Ilie pulled me from the sofa and pushed me into the corridor, shoved a robe at me. The door to the stairs was open.

'Go,' he said.

Ancuta was already halfway down the stairs. I was tying the belt as I went towards her, barefoot, on the cold wooden steps. At the bottom, just outside, Vali was coming in. He had parked Ilie's BMW, left the engine running.

It was dark, cool, not cold, and I felt like I had just arrived in another country. No one was around and streetlights and shop lights were the only sign of life.

Skinny was following and a new girl, a big girl, Lily, was following her.

Ancuta held open the back door and we three, all in robes, got into the car. It happened in seconds. In a few more seconds the car was moving, Ilie driving, Ancuta in the passenger seat, and Vali going back upstairs.

Skinny seemed to have some idea.

'To Dublin?' she said.

'Yes,' said Ancuta.

A day or so before an asshole had complained I had told him I had HIV. And around that time another asshole said I looked like a drug addict, silent and emotionless, as if I was doped out of my brains, and he could not fuck a girl like that, that he wanted girls to be lively. And around that time another asshole had gripped my breast like a vice and I had screamed too loud at him to 'fuck off'.

Ilie was telling me these things as we left Galway, my sleepy eyes counting yellow streetlights as he talked on and on about the things he was hearing. Skinny was tense beside me, but I did not care. I knew some shit would be talked in the car and that it would probably be about me.

We drove onto the motorway as he talked about being fed up with the problems I was causing him. He asked if I wanted to make any money for myself and I did not answer. I hoped he would just shut up.

Ancuta asked, joined in, said this was a good time to think about the way I was doing things.

'Do you want now to make any money?'

I said, 'No.'

I didn't know what else to say. They kept all the money. If I had said I wanted some, I think they would have killed me. But that was not what they meant. They were making an offer.

'So,' said Ilie, 'you don't want to work for me?'

What could I say?

I said nothing.

We drove for a while longer in total silence. There was some reason for him to go to Dublin, to quickly see someone, probably to get cash or to pay cash to someone. He had decided, by whatever method he used, it was better for him to bring three girls with him and Ancuta rather than leave us there. So here I was, a passenger, on a 3.30am road trip to Dublin on the M6 motorway.

It was comfortable in the car, cool, and, apart from Ilie's storytelling, it was quiet. After a while he stopped. I remember feeling myself drifting off to sleep, out of complete necessity, because I was sleeping only maybe one or two hours at a time. My brain wasn't working well, was starting to get all out of shape, was picturing things and saying things that came from nowhere. I remember hoping a large animal would run out in front of us and that we would swerve and all get killed. I remember some crazy stuff about a head-on crash, about hoping that we were going on the wrong road so a big car would suddenly appear going the other way and kill us all. I would laugh at the last second, just to see the look on Ilie's face, on Ancuta's face. Maybe all of that was a dream.

I opened my eyes when the car pulled in at the side of the road. We sat there for a while, the engine running, and I saw Ilie was looking at me in the mirror. It was like he knew what I had been thinking.

He got out of the car and I felt Skinny tense again beside me. He opened my door and grabbed my hair, pulled me out onto the hard shoulder. He pulled the robe from me and shouted, as loud as I had ever heard anyone shout, 'You blind fucking bitch!'

He grabbed my arm, pulled me behind him, right onto the empty motorway. There were two lanes and he dragged me to the middle of both, to where the white lines were.

He shouted again, 'Stay there!'

I was in lingerie, barefoot, half awake, half alive.

Ilie marched back to the car, calling me a 'blind bitch' or a 'bitch from Sibiu' with every step.

I stood there, maybe not as scared as a normal person might have been, as he took out a cigarette and walked to the front of the BMW. He lit it, watching me.

Ahead of me, the way I faced, was where we had come from. A vehicle was coming, some distance away, a lorry, its lights two dots in the dark. I folded my arms, quivering a little bit because of the cold. I asked myself if he really thought I might stand here and be run over by a lorry, because it seemed so ridiculous. But he liked his drama.

Ilie pulled on his cigarette and said, 'Do you want to work for me? Do you want to make money and work for me? Or do you want this?'

And he motioned towards the truck, the lights getting bigger, coming closer the whole time.

You know, I thought how that truck could kill me and I thought that it would not kill me. I thought that driver would see me far ahead of him and brake, that he would not run over a girl in the middle of the motorway. It seemed to be what Ilie wanted to do to make some kind of a point, but it was not the work of a genius.

I thought I could run towards the truck and scream for help. I thought I could run off the side of the road and into the field. I thought so many things. But the biggest thought was that Ilie – even if no genius – was so angry right now, so serious, so frustrated that I was not being the slave he wanted me to be, that if I did the wrong thing now I would suffer very badly.

The choice I made was, I think, the only choice I could make.

I said, 'Yes.'

He said, 'Okay.'

And he beckoned me towards him.

'You work for me, okay?' he said. 'We will pay you when you pay off your debts. You can make lots of money and have a good life.'

'Okay,' I said, and picked my robe up from the side of the car. Maybe a few seconds later the truck passed, the wind blowing up around us.

They call it black humour when people find a way to laugh at bad things. I would never have thought of myself as having black humour, but I found it when I saw, for the first time, terror in the eyes of Ilie.

Understand that I was living in a situation that was opposite to the situation for the pimps. When they were happy, I was sad or hurt or in trouble. When they were eating I was hungry. When they were shouting I was silent. When I was sore they were drunk. And so when they were afraid, I was having a nice time.

It was July and my teeth were getting very bad. If I touched my tongue to the very back I could feel looseness and cracks, feel as if liquid or pus was coming out when I pressed them. I thought my breath must stink, that I might be getting some sort of disease. But I did not fear disease. I did not fear anything that put assholes off raping me. If my breath stank, it was good. If I looked like I had wounds in my mouth, it was good. No one likes to get close to a dirty mouth.

I can tell you that I was still refusing sex without condoms, still telling asshole after asshole that I was not clean. Most of the time that was okay, but sometimes they would try to trick me, get me to put a condom on them and then snap it off just as they went to enter me. My refusing them just made them want to fight me harder.

So many of these assholes liked the idea of rape and I had to weigh up in my mind so many times if it was worth it. When I didn't resist, it was often easier. But still there were times, and I could not help it, when I would lash out in anger, no matter what my fear was of Ilie, of Ancuta.

One asshole told me how he had married a year before and wasn't happy with his sex life even though he loved his wife. He looked like he was going to cry and wanted to hug. I pushed him away and told him a truth. I said, 'You are a stupid fucking man.'

One asshole once told me he loved me and wanted me to come away with him, to be with him as his lover. He came back again, told me he was ready to take me away to London on a boat, that he could be my pimp and he would make sure I was always okay. I told him he had betrayed me in his mind before he even met me.

One man brought a toy that he said belonged to a relative of his and he wanted to see another woman use it. I told him to stick it up his ass and he was offended.

Did he think in his dreams a girl would want a second-hand sex toy from his family in her body? Well yes, it seems clear that he did. He thought a girl would do that for a few euros.

The mentality does get beyond belief, I think. I could not work it out when some of them brought presents, things like perfume, knickers and pieces of jewellery with no value. And then I did work it out, and I believe they do this because it makes them feel better about themselves.

They rub at your feet as if they are pleasuring you, taking time out of their busy days to give you a nice massage because they are nice people, nice assholes. They stroke your hair and ask if you have been to see some famous cliffs yet in Ireland, or if you like to hear the traditional music in the pubs in Galway. They want to know if you would like to have children, if you want to live in Ireland forever, if it snows all the time in Romania or Poland or Russia or wherever it is they have been told you are from.

All of these things make them feel like they are a kind and considerate lover to you.

One old fool told me to 'lie back and enjoy' as he licked my thighs, vagina, stomach and breasts and all the way up to my neck and face. I could feel my fists clenching as he started licking at my eyes, leaving the stench from his rotten tongue all over my skin. One of my fists flew out, out of nowhere, and hit him on the face. He said he was sorry and left me alone.

There are people, you see, who really believe they are doing you a favour when they are in fact doing themselves the favour. It is as simple as that.

But then they are led to believe all of that, as if just by visiting you they are making you happy. It is how the girls are sold, the PR of the industry.

They are asked to come along and make this happy girl even happier, to give her some money so that you can share pleasure and joy.

And even before you come along, you see, you can pick from the menu of wonderful, fun things you can do.

Many, so many, want OWO.

This is Oral WithOut.

They want their dick in your mouth without a condom. It is disgusting, but I could not always fight against what so many wanted. My only choice was to pick my battles carefully as I could not fight with them all.

The shyer ones, if they ask for it, you say, 'No.' The rougher ones, you might have to just go ahead, because you do not want them to force it.

And sometimes you just get a feeling, an inkling, an instinct, that you can work them into a frenzy before they even ask for it, that you can make them cum in seconds by giving them the least amount of yourself.

The handjob does not always work, but if you just go ahead and reach for it sometimes the man will just sit back. A successful handjob is a victory in this disgusting world.

But back to OWO. Do you want OWO? Well, if so, remember you can check the details on the girl's profile to see if she will. And if she is trafficked, as so very many are, of course she will. It will be there, even if the girl does not know what it means. Because the girl did not write that profile herself.

Or you can see if she does:

COB – Cum on Body; 69; anal receiving; anal giving; couples; deep-throat; fingering; facial – cum on face; uniforms; strap-on; sex toys; role play.

You can see if it's okay to wear knickers and a bra when you visit, see if she will play the game when you are wearing your wife's, friend's or daughter's underwear.

Watersports – peeing; French kissing; rimming – licking the ass; spanking; handjob; tea-bagging – balls into the girl's mouth;

strap-on; shared showers; Russian – sex between the breasts; hardsports – pooing.

And many more.

It is like browsing in a shop window to see which secret you want to have come true with the magical fantasy girl who waits only to please, who wants to have your balls or your shit in her mouth, who wants only for you to slap her and abuse her for the cost of a bicycle for a child.

There are couples too, men and women who enquire and ask to meet with one girl or two girls. Men like to see their girl with another girl, doing what he wants them to do for the right price.

And there are – once in a while – lone women too, mostly just those who ring and ask out of curiosity and then do not arrive. But there are women who want to spend time with a girl, always on out-calls to hotels or houses. For some girls that is a good thing and a bad thing. It is good in that a woman is not likely to hurt them, to abuse them, to stick things into her that she does not want. But at the same time a woman likes more to be touched, to be consoled, to be loved, and by a girl who has nothing she has. These women must have some feminine understanding of what it must be to be a sex slave.

The women must be able to understand, just as the men must be able to understand, if they thought about it clearly for just a few minutes, that fantasy takes place within reality, that someone is paying a price for pleasure of any kind on demand and the price is not just in money. Fantasy using trafficked women is fundraising for pimps and nothing more. It is fantasy happening while the Mother Pimp takes out a whole bin of used condoms every day, where she puts bleach in soap dishes and tells girls to wash with it. It is fantasy taking place near an empty fridge and always just a few minutes from violence in some way or other.

We drank strong coffee and sometimes Ilie would splash whisky in, as if he was being a gentleman. We never had cooked food made in that flat, or at least nothing more than a bowl of beans. There were no pictures on the walls and they never liked to open windows. It was a farm, a factory, a place of work where you did not even know who wanted to be there, who had been stolen, who would cause you trouble or hit you or tell stories about you to someone else. We lived inches from each other, naked, hungry, empty inside, and we also lived a hundred miles from each other.

Some girls asked for drugs and flirted with Ilie to help them be successful. Some girls wanted vodka, some wanted cigarettes, some just wanted make-up and to work all the time, non-stop, as much as they could.

Skinny was the smallest of all the girls, the prettiest too, and she could never get enough drink, never enough cocaine into her little body. This girl was a child, but she and I were so popular with the customers that we were precious to Ilie and the Mother Pimp.

We spoke a few times in our time together, but only once did we have an important conversation. We usually spoke nonsense about the heat in the flat and the crap shower, we spoke about how much sleep we had and if the coffee was very strong. We spoke about our love of sleep, of what we would give for a long night in a comfortable bed with a sea breeze blowing around us.

She was from a poor village near Bucharest and her boyfriend there had groomed her so well. He had brought her to Bucharest and let her get stars tattooed on her hand and this had made her feel like she was becoming a woman, a star, in her own little life, that she was becoming something from nothing. He said he could fix her up with some webcam work and it would be great for both of them, that they could both make good money and live a wonderful, happy life.

From there she was flown to Ireland, aged 17, and was told her boyfriend would join her soon. And, she told me, she was still waiting for him. There had been, she said, a mix-up over the webcam work and the escort work and she had ended up doing the second one.

You know, the girl just did not understand. She had been told a long time ago, she said, by her boyfriend, if anyone ever asked, to always say she was only doing webcam work. And she stuck to that promise, she said, for as long as anyone could.

I wanted to hug Skinny, but I never did. I never became that close with her. Because after we had talked about her life, Skinny talked to Ancuta. I don't know why. I don't know if Ancuta told her to speak about it or if Skinny had volunteered. But anyway she told Mother Pimp all about what we had talked about and Ancuta slapped my face so many times.

Skinny's story was not my business, she said. I had no business to ask about hers. Everyone has their privacy, she said, and no one must ask to know anyone else's story.

It was funny though, because Skinny would become very much my business. She was, I am glad to tell you, not going to be a fool forever.

Ilie sometimes made it seem as if he liked us all, as if he was choosing not to rape us out of respect. We all had to suck Vali's dick, with no condom, and we had all had to suck Carol's dick too, under Ancuta's orders, with no condom, before he returned to London. But we never had to do that with Ilie.

When Ancuta was near to him, he was not so nice to any of us and liked to turn his nose up, to show in some way that we disgusted him. She would watch him, to see if his eyes were spending too long on one girl or another. And I tell you that he liked to look at me a lot, to offer me things he had – whisky, food, cigarettes – and Ancuta did not like that at all.

There were a few times when I saw Ancuta cry, but just quickly and just to let a few tears out so she could then move on. She would drink so much and talk to herself and shove the girls around and slap faces and sometimes a little tear would show.

I am not asking you to have some sympathy for this woman. I do not have words for how much of a bitch this woman is. I am just asking you to know that even she, in her shit position in this shit business, knew in her black heart it was based so much on unhappiness. To be a pimp, to make sex customers happy 24 hours a day, you need to be a person who manages the unhappiness of other people and that unhappiness can only be infectious.

But fear is a different thing. Fear is what they use to control you and it brought me real joy to see her in fear, to see Ilie in fear, to see Vali in fear. And this is the black humour I told you about.

It happened this way: Ancuta cleared some girls from a room, waved her hand in front of my face and told me to get ready. I touched up my face, went into the room, straightened up the covers on the bed and sat down. I was wearing my lingerie.

There were big, heavy footsteps and she led a large man into the room. And I mean a large man, the biggest man I had ever seen. He had a beard, and was wearing a black jacket, a blue shirt and some dark trousers. He was drunk, very drunk, and bashed himself into the frame of the door as he came in.

Ancuta nodded at me, the way she always did, and closed the door. The man waved me off the bed and I stood up. He sat down and I could smell every part of him. He was not clean. He had little bits of food or dirt around his mouth. His feet were stinking even though his dirty shoes were still on. I had smelled this kind of man many times before, but because he was so big it was like the smell was bigger too.

He said something in a very Irish accent and I didn't know for sure what it was, but I think he asked me for a glass of water. I stood and just watched him as he closed his eyes and began to fall back onto the bed. He was, you know, bigger than the bed. His stomach could have held 10 footballs.

His feet were like a giant's.

I stood back and watched him go off to sleep. He was snoring very quickly and I didn't know what to do. As I looked at him I could see a lot of his belly and that there was a knife there, which had been hidden under his jacket, sticking up above his belt. It was in a holder that was tucked into the inside of his trousers.

I could not just sit here and wait for this man to have his sleep. I opened the door and there was no one in the corridor. The door to the living room was closed and it was quiet. The other bedroom was busy and the door was closed.

This was the first time in all that time that I thought to myself, 'What about going out of the exit door?'

It was noisy – I knew it made a big click when the latch was opened and the door was pulled – but I wondered if I could do it quietly. And then what? Down the wooden stairs? Opening the other door? Onto the street? Would it be busy at this time? What will happen if I am stopped?

I could hear now an asshole moaning in the other bedroom and the big man in my room snoring.

Where would I go? Would they run after me and catch me? Would I be able to find someone to listen to me in my lingerie? What would I say to them in my Romanian accent?

And I was standing at that door in the quiet corridor, and I had my hands on the cold latch that I had never touched before.

I felt my heart beating hard, a heartbeat I had not felt in a while because I was so used to this life. One little turn and before it even opened it made a squeak sound, a little sound like from a mouse.

I froze on the spot, I can tell you. I stood like a statue, listening to everything. And I heard some talking in the living room and I knew someone was coming. Maybe it was the sound of a chair moving or the way someone had spoken, but I knew someone was coming to the living-room door.

It opened and Ancuta was looking at me. And now I was standing right in front of her, turned away from the door, facing the living-room door. She looked at me and the exit door and then at me again.

'He has fallen asleep,' I said.

'Did he do anything?'

'No. He just lay down and fell asleep. He has a knife in his belt.'

She turned and told Ilie and everyone in the living room what I had said. She came out into the corridor and pushed me back into the bedroom.

'This is bullshit,' she said. She called Ilie. We all stood over the man, looking at his size, at the knife in his belt.

Ilie asked Ancuta if he was a Traveller and she said she thought he was.

'Okay,' he said. 'This might be a problem. We will have to try to get him out.'

He got Vali and Makar, another pimp who was in the living room that night. They were both drunk. They all tried to lift the Traveller but it was a struggle for them. I stood against a wall and watched as they tried to pick him up in different ways, but it was no good. He was a huge rock.

Ancuta had to help too and she could hardly lift any part of this man. 'We will have to wake him up,' she said.

'No,' said Ilie. 'We have to get him out and away from here.'

I didn't understand their concern, but it was making me smile. They had a big, stinking problem on their hands and they didn't know what to do. It was the first difficulty I had ever seen them have.

'Blind one,' Ancuta said, 'go to the living room.'

A phone call was made and maybe twenty minutes later two other pimps arrived. The phones rang but they were not answered. This was an emergency meeting about the Traveller man.

They all went to him and the sound of grunting and bashing and banging went on for five minutes as they carried the big man into the corridor and down the little stairs and out onto the street. I was later told that they put him onto the ground in a park or on a pavement somewhere. They just wanted so very badly to get him out of there.

Ancuta stayed behind and started answering phones again and drinking wine and smoking. When the men came back they looked as if they had been in a war and worry was all over their faces.

They feared this was a man they had heard about. They feared he had been hired to come and do some damage to their business, to make a threat, to cause a problem. This man was a man who they were sure was linked to some Travellers in Dublin who Ilie had fallen out with maybe a year ago. Ilie had owed money to pimps in Dublin before he left for Galway. A group of Traveller men, who were maybe being paid by pimps, had kidnapped him near Dublin Airport and brought him to a house for questioning. Ilie had been beaten up and burned with an iron in a hotel. He escaped only when he promised to pay off what he owed.

The men drank more and talked more about their concerns. They said they felt the attention was again turning to them, to Ilie. He was ghost white as they talked about how the man might have been there to kill me or Skinny because the pimps knew we had both been making so much money. He told me himself that the big man would be wanting to make things very bad for us, and that could mean anything.

It was maybe 24 hours later when panic came among the pimps again. The same very big man was seen in the street close to the brothel and walking around and talking on his mobile phone. Ilie was shaking with fear when he heard this in a phone call from another man. Ancuta was smoking and drinking at the same time and wanted to know what Ilie knew.

I was sitting on the little sofa and I had a smile as big as a banana. It was funny for me. The other girls there were confused, looking at me and smiling and trying to work out what this was. I put my head down and I chuckled. I was just waiting for a hand to slap me so hard and I didn't care.

Ilie looked all around him, at his girls, at the room, and said, 'We have to go.'

Chapter Fourteen

All pimps who come to Ireland from Romania and other countries know about Galway. They have friends, cousins, contacts in the city who will be able to help them get into business. In Dublin it is harder; the business is controlled by a lot of different gangs and it can be very violent, very threatening for new people to get a foothold without crossing the wrong people. But in Galway it is easier. There is so much passing trade, so many people involved in the sex business who arrive one day and move on the next, that there is less trouble. For the size of the city, the sex trade in Galway is very big and all the pimps are making money.

Ilie did not have to take us far. He was not giving up on his little base above the bookies because it was a good place for business, but he was moving his girls and his computers out of it for now. And when he wanted to make changes, to move things or people or money around, he did not waste time. He travelled light and fast, a way of doing things that I would get to know well, and he would never explain what was going on.

Vali gathered up laptops and mobile phones and Ancuta gathered clothes, her make-up, the packets of condoms and a bag of cleaning products and other pieces. We were told to get our things, which was simple, and she gave out some shirts and robes to wear. We looked like we were leaving a party that had been broken up. Late at night, girls in underwear with maybe just a jacket over their almost naked bodies, running fast down the stairs.

If I tell you that I was scared, it will probably sound stupid. You would think I was already living in hell and how could I be scared of anything now? But the hell I knew was at least known to me. I thought how any change could make things worse and make me have to start all over again, trying to use my environment and skills and knowledge of the property to try to make things better.

Ilie was first to leave and then Vali. Then they both came back. They came into the room and ushered us to them. We made our way out behind them, myself and Skinny and two other girls – Lily and Rena – and behind all of us was Ancuta. She was saying, 'Go on, go on, go on,' as all our feet were rumbling down the steps.

At the bottom, the door was open onto the street and two cars were parked there. Ancuta pushed and Ilie and Vali pulled and in maybe five seconds we were all in the cars, cold, knowing nothing, our hearts beating hard. The streetlights were on but, as before, I don't remember seeing anyone, really seeing anything. I had an instinct it was late, maybe midnight, maybe 2am, but I couldn't know. I did try to look at the clock in the car from the back seat, just to see if I could learn that detail, but stretching your neck to look at the wrong thing was not a good idea. I had learned a special type of body language and it was to keep myself as small and still as possible. Anyway, it did not matter.

It only took five minutes to get there. I know now, about Galway, that Ilie had so many contacts there that he could arrange for a new place in a few minutes. From what I know, he had friends in the property market, estate agents, landlords, who asked few questions when he explained he did all his business by cash.

In five minutes we were at Merchants Quay, right in the city centre, and being pushed and pulled upstairs and into an apartment. It was all furnished and nice, but cold and stale as no one had been in there for a while.

The first thing that happened was for Vali to find the kitchen, to put down his computers, switch them on and see what he was going to do about getting an internet connection. Ilie helped him. Before they even walked around the place, they were trying to make sure they could do business. Selling sex was their obsession. It got them money, which was their drug Men who want money more than they want anything else are the worst kind of men, the most dangerous kind, because nothing but money has value to them.

Ancuta had us all putting bedclothes on, making up rooms. And as soon as she was done, she started answering the calls again. She stood in front of me, fixing her hair, pulling it back and looking in a mirror.

'Yes, darling,' she said, 'do you know where Merchants Quay is? Yes, my darling. That's where you will find me.'

There was no break in business. It was like a very fast scenery change in a play on the stage.

I used the bathroom and saw it was bigger than the one in the other place. The rooms were bigger and more modern. There was more carpet in there than we had before. There were two bedrooms, as before, and one had a little balcony. There was a nice, clean, white kitchen, bigger than before. It was a good apartment, but to me it looked only like a new prison, a new zoo, a different place for lying assholes to come to visit and grab and screw and insult us.

And everything changed and nothing changed. Ilie felt he was safer – him, not us – and Ancuta thought she was moving up in the world. The assholes were the same and the days were the same. If you ask me to tell you about who came to visit in the first day or the second day, I can't tell you. I can't remember. I can't tell you the difference between one day above the bookies and one day beside the sea. It was the same. The hatred for me was the same, the abuse of my body was the same.

It was in this place that I turned 22. I thought about my mother on that day. It was 16 July 2011. Ancuta told me it was my birthday. She told me to go into the bathroom and said she was going to dye my hair. I didn't ask why. I was past asking why. I was thin and quiet and not very responsive to anything at all.

So she got to work on my hair, pressing my head down to wet it and to add the stuff she needed to add. I did not even look.

And after she was finished it was jet black. So for the first time in my life my hair wasn't blonde. It was also longer than it had been maybe since I was a little girl.

She tied it up in a towel and washed the stains off my neck and shoulders. In the mirror in that bathroom, with my hair black, I could see that my shape had changed. I had gone, you know, from a size 10–12 to a size 6, in such a short time. I was getting no exercise, no fresh air, no food that was of any use to my body. I was in the worst physical state of my life. Making my hair different for assholes was so unimportant I cannot even say.

When it was dry she had me put on my new red lingerie and the brown Primark robe she had gifted me after I agreed, on the motorway, I would work for Ilie. I went to a room. And all the time she was saying, 'Happy birthday,' and smiling as if she meant it.

I could not have cared if I was 22 or 122.

She let two Russian assholes into the room and closed the door. They were maybe late twenties and I think they were high or maybe just crazy. They did not waste any of their time. They wanted to get on with this.

And this is what happened. They pulled me up and stripped me off. Before I was even laid back on the bed, a hand over my mouth, I was being assaulted hard, everywhere. And when I was on the bed they put everything inside me – fingers, fists, feet – and raped me everywhere as hard as they could. They punched me and spat on me, they hit my ears and nose and head and bit my breasts.

It maybe took 20 minutes, but I don't remember it so well. Sometimes the brain does not want to keep all the memories.

After they left, I couldn't move. I was sore everywhere – my face, eyes, teeth, head, body, organs, skin. My eyes were closed for a long time because it was a kind of comfort, the only kind of comfort I could get, which is something I cannot explain. I could not really feel about half of my stomach inside, like it was numb. My body, as it often did, had opposed everything but there was no way for me to prevent what was happening.

Ancuta told me to get up. She said she would fix the bed and I had to shower, to use cold water so the bruises would maybe not be as bad. She said she had a cookie for me for my birthday. It was hard to know sometimes if she was saying something out of hate or as a joke or if she was serious. But that's what she said. And she did have a cookie for me. 'There's your cookie,' she said, and I had to catch it when she threw it.

I think the Russians might have been pimps, people involved in the same business, because Ancuta seemed happy to please them, not troubled that they had been so vicious. They were, you know, not too far from killing me.

I sat on the toilet after it all and didn't know what would happen, what might come out of my insides. I was swelling up badly and, as she had said, I did find myself putting the cold tap on to see if I could help keep the bruises down. I thought that I would never be healthy again. I thought this was it. I thought I must be coming to some kind of end of my life. I could not swallow well for days after that day because it was like my neck had been crushed.

If you meet me and it is my birthday, please don't say it.

It was nine days later when Ancuta walked out quickly. I can tell you I know for sure it was nine days because my birthday was on 16 July and the police raid was on 25 July. It was a busy time because the Galway Races were just beginning, which is such a big event in the city.

There were more assholes ringing in than I had ever seen before and Ancuta and Ilie did not want to miss one of them.

I don't know how many people come to the horse racing but it seemed like all of Ireland was there. The assholes would come in drunk with rolls of notes and tell me they hoped I would bring them luck.

I said I had only no luck and bad luck and they thought it was funny, that I was having fun with them. The inside of an asshole's head when he is having his fantasy is not a place where you can change anything easily.

Some of them smelled of horses, of farms, of brandy and shit. Some smelled of expensive cologne and wore only brand-new clothes. They all smiled a lot, all seemed happy and comfortable because they were on a break or at their favourite event in the calendar. They were from all over Ireland, from England, Scotland and everywhere, and some of the accents were impossible for me to understand.

And then one night, I don't know what time, when one asshole had just left me, I went into the shower. As the water was tumbling down, just after I had washed some filth from my hair, there was noise outside. It was a shouting and a banging. I stopped the water so I could hear it clearly.

'Don't move!'

'Stay there!'

'Go there!'

Men and women shouting. People did sometimes shout in our world, but not like this. It was a thundering of footsteps, like an army of people crashing into some place. I was listening and not having any idea of what was happening. And the bathroom door was pushed open and one and two and three and four and,

I think, seven people were coming in and filling the space and looking around and putting their hands up to me to tell me not to move.

'Stay where you are!' someone said.

All blue uniforms, the blue of the gardaí, the Irish police force.

'Don't move!'

I was not going to move. I was naked, dripping from the shower, stuck to the spot.

And then there was a time, maybe a short time, but a time that I can remember clearly. A moment, a few seconds, where all of these people were looking at me, up and down, at my body, at the bruises on my skin, my breasts and legs, at the damaged woman in front of them. And the faces, at least some of the faces, were looking at me not with a horror or a surprise or sympathy but with only disgust.

I'm telling you I remember that moment because I can recall the looks so well. I was used to assholes looking at me with lust or desire or that sex rage face they get when they want to hurt you, to do hard things to you. And these were different looks. These were not looks of pity, of sadness or kindness, not the looks of police officers finding a crime. These were the looks a child gives when he does not like his soup or a woman gives when she steps in something that stinks. In that little moment I was more surprised by their looks than I was at their being there.

Someone said they were from the police and I could hear more of them running around in the apartment shouting at the other three girls.

'You are all under arrest,' said one of them, one of the disgusted faces.

And I said, 'That's fine.'

And what I meant was I have no argument with you. What I meant was that's fine if you want to take me away. I was saying no problem. I was saying you have found me. You have found what you will call a prostitute but what you have found is a woman who has been kidnapped. You have found a trafficked woman, a slave, who does not want to be in this place any more than you do. And what I meant was that now I was going to be able to tell them all about it. What I meant was take me away because you can make me free.

A policewoman handed me a towel, her fingers just gripping the edge of it, and let go just as I reached out to grab it, maybe in case I infected her with the touch of my skin. But I was still glad they were there. I was thinking I would cover myself up and go with them to talk.

'Thank you,' I said but she did not smile.

None of them smiled. They all watched as I put the towel around myself.

Chapter Fifteen

We were allowed to get some clothing. They took us in two cars to the police station. But it took time to be brought out of that flat because first they sat us down on the sofa to ask us a hundred things.

'Do you speak English?'

'No,' the other workers said.

'Yes,' I said.

One of them – police officers – grabbed me by the hands and said loudly, maybe shouted, into my face, 'Who are you? Who are you?'

I said my name, my real full name, and he was not listening. He did the same to Skinny, 'Who are you?!'

She was shaking.

Another one started.

He shouted about the computers, the laptops, where had they all gone?

He looked at me: 'Where?!'

I did not know. The others – Skinny, Rena and Lily – could understand too and said they did not know. More shouts, more of a kind of pressure that there was no need to place on us.

What about the cash? I didn't know where the cash was. We didn't know. I just assumed it had gone because Ancuta had also gone. 'We don't get the cash,' I said.

One said, 'You are in charge, aren't you?'

I said no, I was not in charge.

The other girls were shaking their heads; they said, 'She is not in charge.' And they were shaking their heads back like they were mocking.

They were gathering up phones, lots of phones. Some were ringing as they packed them up to take them away as live evidence, buzzing, flashing proof of this being a brothel. There could be no doubt. They took photographs of condoms, of used condoms, of the rooms, of us, of underwear, of the wires on the wall where the laptops had been.

Ancuta and Ilie and Vali had cleared out fast. How fast do you have to be when 20 police are coming for you? How fast would they have to have been to get out before so many police arrived? It felt to me as if they knew before the police were at the door, before they were on the street.

I have never known the answer. But I do know that the four of us girls they arrested that day, who were given our rights as we sat in the place where no rights existed, were not the criminals.

Lily, you must know, hated that world and wanted to go home, but did what she was told. Skinny hated it too but, as you know, was loyal to Ilie and Ancuta and did what she was told. Rena did the work too, hated the place too, hated the assholes too, but did what she was told. And me, I did the work too and hated the assholes and, most of the time, I did what I was told.

Maybe the only true difference is that all three of those women were tricked, but I was not. They were groomed and caught in the trap, when I was never groomed. I was just stolen.

Lily was a taller girl, a curvy girl, and they wanted to keep her after she was brought by a pimp to the flat above the bookies. She was liked by tall men and by men who like bigger bottoms. Rena was slender, a brunette, and also liked by men who like certain things. And Skinny was just skinny, just tiny, just a scared child for assholes to abuse. She was an important part of the horrible little empire Ilie was trying to build.

But none of our stories mattered now. We were arrested and were taken to a police station and were locked into cells, the same place every criminal goes.

In a while I was brought to be questioned by a detective. A solicitor was there to meet me, to tell me who he was, that he was representing me. I do not think he even looked at my face.

The detective said, 'Where are your documents? Any ID, passport?'

I said I didn't know, that they had been taken and kept by the pimps.

He asked me fast questions. He asked did I know Ancuta Schwarz and Ilie Ionut, and I said I did and I had seen them that day. I said Ancuta lived in the flat and Ilie was often there. He asked who else I knew and I said I had seen lots of people. He asked how did my English get so good and I said I could speak good English before I moved to London. He asked for my details and I gave them to him. I told him my name, my real name, and my date of birth and where I was from.

He said, 'Yes, you're the one who rented the apartment.'

'I am sorry? Rented what apartment?'

'Merchants Quay,' he said. 'It's rented in your name.'

'I didn't know that.'

'No,' he said, 'of course not.'

My details were on the documents as the renter of the apartment, not those of Ilie or Ancuta. They had used my ID without my knowledge.

'I am not a prostitute,' I said.

'You will be in court in the morning,' he said.

The solicitor said, 'It will be a brief hearing and a fine. You will be free to go after that.'

'Free to go?' I said.

'Yes,' he said. 'It's not a big deal. Girls and pimps often get arrested at the time of the Galway Races. It looks good. It's nothing to worry about.'

I asked, 'Can I phone my mother?'

'After court,' he said.

And that was it.

I was taken back to my cell where I sat, starving and exhausted and full of questions.

Free? What did that mean? Free to go and walk somewhere on my own, to make phone calls? Free? I didn't know what I would do first.

In the morning they drove us from the police station to the court. The police told all of us not to say a word, that we would be in and out and there would be nothing to worry about.

All of us were taken to the dock early in the morning, maybe 9am, and asked to give our names.

I could have said I was the King of Spain or Margaret Thatcher because no one looked at me. They didn't even have my papers. But I said my name again and I could see that there was a person writing it all down, someone in the court writing my name, and I liked to see that happening. Maybe I thought somewhere in my mind it was like a bit of a trail, a bit of evidence that I had been there.

So this is the report of the hearing from that day that was in a local paper:

> Four women who were convicted of running a brothel in an apartment in Galway City centre this week have each been fined €300.
>
> The women, aged between 19 and 23, pleaded guilty to assisting in the management of the brothel at Merchants Road when they appeared before the District Court this morning.
>
> The brothel, which was being advertised on the internet, was raided by gardaí last night.
>
> During the raid they found 21 mobile phones, details of clients and €1,500 in cash in the apartment ...
>
> Judge Aeneas McCarthy told gardaí, who sought to have the women deported, that he did not have the jurisdiction to do so.

So you think the police knew that this judge could not deport us? I think so. It was a stupid thing to ask. All he could do was let us go.

Do you think they took the 21 mobile phones and explored them for evidence? Do you think they went on to build a case against the sex underworld in Galway? Do you think that they thought the 1,500 euros – wherever they found it – was all there was to be seized?

No, no and no.

We signed something and were escorted out of the courtroom. As we came to the exit door we were looking at each other, quiet, uncertain, confused. It was strange, like a dream, that we were walking into a bright morning, four girls who wanted nothing more in the world than a brighter day.

Chapter Sixteen

We were four foreign, unslept women, four women with slow, sore bodies and very little hope in our hearts. But we had spent some time together, got to know each other a little, been through something together without our every move being watched, without having to suck dicks or do what Ancuta told us. It was a strange time.

There was Skinny, the tricked and trafficked 19-year-old. There was Lily, 22, the curvy one who cried all the time. There was Rena, 23, the unhappy slender one who was always being told to wear long boots by assholes. And there was me, 22, the stolen cleaner, the one who once dreamed of dispensing psychology, the one now in the middle of a city she had lived in for months but had never seen.

What a sight we would have been. If my grandmother had seen these four girls walking out of the courthouse looking like what we had been told we legally were – prostitutes – she would have shouted across the street, 'You have no self-respect!' But we did have self-respect, it is just that it had been lost under all the hatred and anger and mind games and hunger games that we had been taking part in.

All of where we had been and what we had learned was at the front of our minds on that day because suddenly what lay ahead was not clear.

And now I can tell you two feelings that happened at the same time, which might confuse you as they confused me. One – I hated Ilie and Ancuta and Vali with everything I had. I wanted them to die. Two – I felt scared, very deep down and only for a few moments, because they were not there.

That might be hard to understand, but it is something I have now come to terms with, some kind of strange security found from being in prison, like that insane thing, Stockholm Syndrome, kidnapped people slip into when they bond with their captors. When you have lost faith in yourself I think you will find it in the strangest places, and I think – even though I knew it was the most stupid thing in the world – that I had been given a routine, a set of dependencies, and was so used to it that being free from it would take some adjusting to.

So there we were, coming out of the court, arrested, charged and fined and the pimps had got totally away.

And then I had what they call a reality check. I realised I no longer had to even think about any of that, about freedom, about the world I was walking into. For Ilie and Ancuta and Vali were right there, outside the court, waiting to pick us up.

'In,' they said, holding the car doors open.

And do you know what we did? Yes, we got in.

The two cars, both BMWS, took us back to Merchants Quay. The place had been destroyed by the police. Stuff was everywhere. Ancuta said to grab everything – bedding and towels and make-up and perfumes and condoms – and put it all into the cars. Then we were told to get back in because we were leaving.

We drove straight out of Galway and onto the motorway, which took us east, and then north towards Northern Ireland.

Ancuta was in the passenger seat, looking at me and Skinny in the back seat.

'What did they ask you?'

Skinny shrugged and I shrugged.

I said, 'Nothing. They just talked.'

'How much were you fined?'

'I don't know.'

'Did you tell them your name?'

'Yes.'

She shook her head, as if I was stupid or as if I had done something wrong.

'We are going to Belfast,' she said, turning back around to face the front again. 'We need to get away from all of this.'

Ilie said, 'You have to make some money. We have lost so much money that we will all suffer now.'

I looked out the window at the fields.

There is a café, a motorway services centre, on the M1 towards Northern Ireland, called Applegreen. Ilie and Vali pulled in there to get fuel. They told us to get out when they parked up.

We were walked inside. This is a big complex, a shop, café and a coffee bar and some fast food places and toilets. They took seats and Ancuta went to order food. I felt as shit as I looked and needed to go to the toilet.

'Just go,' said Ilie, pointing.

I walked to the bathroom and looked at the people all around me, getting breakfast and reading newspapers and talking on their phones.

In the bathroom I thought, 'What should I do now?'

I was going again to another city I didn't know, but one where I knew of course I would be watched all the time, where I would be raped all the time. I was so tired, tired in every part of my brain and body, so, so tired, exhausted just trying to think of what I was doing, of what was happening.

What if I was to walk out of the door and keep walking?

What if I was to go to one of the staff there and say, 'Please can you help me?'

So tell me something, now that you know how tired I was, now that you know I had learned a lot about what it is to be a girl in a situation like that – tell me what would you have done?

You see, I have been asked this question before. And it is a good question, unless you have any tiny idea about what it is like to be in that position.

You want me to explain?

If I walked out the door and kept walking I would be in the middle of nowhere, in a county on the coast of Ireland where I knew no one. How long would it be before Ilie walked out of the same door and got me?

If I had run out the door, I would have been in the same place. And again, how long before Ilie, before Vali got me?

If I went up to staff and said I needed help, I would be talking to someone who knew nothing about me. How long would it be before Ilie got me? How long before Vali or Ancuta came along and explained that I was just a fool, to forget about it?

In any case I was a convicted prostitute, a Romanian girl in Ireland with no money doing something stupid that no one wanted to help her with.

And in every case I would have been punched in the car until I was sick, and I would have to clean it up.

If you have other suggestions on how I should have got free that day, you must tell me. Because I was NEVER thinking about doing that! Do you understand me? Do you understand how sarcastic I can get about this?

I left the bathroom, my hands and face washed, hair fixed, and wandered back over in my sweatpants and shirt and slippers to the table where they sat.

I was offered a burger. They were all eating burgers, all hungry and chewing them like starving animals, their mouths munching the only sound. And I ate like an animal. I was so hungry that I had been about to fall over and maybe not be able to get up.

We drove to Belfast, which took maybe an hour. On the way, Ancuta turned to me, laughing. She had my glasses in her hand, the arms folded in, and she reached over with them and said, 'Here you are, blind one. Look what I found.'

This filled my heart with some kind of excitement. It is hard for me to explain. But I took them from her and turned them over in my hand. She turned back round and didn't care.

Skinny looked at me, smiling, and I slowly put the glasses on. And it was incredible, a real moment of positive change at a time of only negative change.

'Is it better?' said Skinny.

'Yes,' I said, 'much better.'

And it was better, but it was not perfect. I knew then that my sight was now even worse because before my glasses had allowed me to see everything, and this time they allowed me to see more but not all. Yet I am telling you I was happy to have something I knew, anything, from the times before. Putting on my glasses made me feel better.

Ancuta and Ilie talked for a while about the raid, about the 1,500 euros that had been seized. They seemed puzzled, as if they had no idea whose it was or where it had been found. I think what they said was that there could not have been any money there, that a run had been made to Western Union with a lot of cash from Ireland days before. They could not work out the story behind the money and, in truth, they did not care.

Twenty-one mobile phones had also been taken. Details of calls and numbers would be on the SIM cards. And that did not bother Ancuta or Ilie either. The phones were unregistered. The only numbers on there were those of assholes, and they did not care about them. They were going now to find new assholes to not care about.

I could look at the roads better now, at the signs with the names of Irish towns. It made me think of an Irish pub in Sibiu where they have food and fiddle music and pictures of U2 and leprechauns. I tried to hold the names of the towns in my head. Drogheda, Dundalk, Newry, Banbridge, Lisburn, Belfast.

We came into the city centre in the afternoon and parked up on a road with tall buildings called Adelaide Street.

Ilie went to meet someone as we sat in the car looking at the people who walked past. The car filled with smoke and Ancuta looked at her phone. Vali came up to the car and said it was time to get out.

We stood on the street and he pointed us towards a big apartment building called Margarita Plaza. Ancuta handed us stuff to carry and Vali pointed.

'Go,' he said, 'Ilie is there. Bring everything.'

Ilie had met with someone, had a discussion and arranged for us to get a two-bedroom place inside.

A man was standing holding the door open when we came up, helping to usher us inside. Ilie was walking around, checking it over, looking out of the windows.

'It's fine,' he said to me, to all of us.

And you know what happened? Yes, they plugged in the laptops and went to work. They changed the city on the profiles, switched the prices from euros to pounds – and let anyone who was looking for sex know that we were new in town, that we were sexy fresh meat with great reviews who just wanted to do everything with the men of Belfast.

Here's a little trick that they did. I came to learn this. You have five girls as prostitutes in one apartment – Ancuta was also for sale – but they did not advertise five girls. They advertised maybe 10 or 15 girls. They take your picture in a different way against a different background. They get you to lie on the bed and turn your head away. They change the angles, sometimes show the face, sometimes not. They take pictures of you with your breasts showing and then pictures of you with a coloured bra. They change your hair, your make-up. They make you become Rona and Zelda and Ana and Anica and Liliana and Rachel and Ruby and Natalia and Natasha. They make you from Romania and Poland and Ukraine and Russia and Latvia because none of that matters because all that matters is that you have a female body.

And yes my picture was taken many times. It was taken and edited and glossed and airbrushed and sometimes you would think I was living in a palace and that I dreamed only of sex with random Irish men who had some notes and 10 minutes to spare on their way home from work. What a fantasy I was. I was porn and I could come to life and I was so close to where you are now.

When the assholes came, I could not know if I was Ana or Natalia or Ruby and I did not care. They would say, 'Hi, Anica, I have a friend from Ukraine, where you're from,' as if I gave a shit about any of this. Not even they gave a shit about any of this.

Never once did I hear any asshole go, 'Hey, you are not from Czech Republic like it says on your profile,' or, 'Hey, you are the same girl as Helena with different clothes!' That does not happen when the assholes arrive. Those details are not important when they are about to have sex with a stranger.

So Ilie would make sure we were all advertised again and again and again as different girls but all available at the same time. This means that the assholes have – or think they have – more choice all the time.

'No,' they say to themselves as they look at the website, 'I don't like this Karina from Poland instead I like this Sofia from Russia.' And she is the same girl.

I don't know what my names were in Belfast. I had so many names. It didn't matter. The men arrived that day, maybe two hours after we arrived, and the routine began again. Hungry, tired, thirsty, raped, all at the same time, over and over.

*

Ancuta flip-flopped to me and handed over some toast and butter. She said to Ilie, behind her, 'The blind one can see better now.'

He said, 'She is the best at English.'

I chewed on my toast, my legs crossed, wondering what they were talking about.

'You can answer the phones,' Ancuta said. And I stopped chewing.

Ilie looked over. 'Can you answer the phones properly and make us all happy?'

I started chewing again.

Ancuta gave me a phone.

'It's one phone for Skinny,' she said. 'Be nice and call them "baby" and tell them Adelaide Street, okay?'

'Okay,' I said.

'And when they come they ring you back and you say Margarita Plaza.'

'Okay,' I said.

The men would be buzzed in from the front door when they said they were there. Up they would come in the lift and knock on the door. It would be opened, usually by Ancuta, who would take the money and show them into the room.

When she was doing that, she said, I could be taking more calls.

'It's best for everyone,' she said. 'You can speak to them the best, keep them interested. Wear more make-up, you feel better talking on the phone. And we can both take all the calls because it will be busy, okay?'

I said, 'Okay.'

I tell you this, I had a lot of thinking to do.

Would it be true that if I was sending the assholes to other girls they would not be abusing me? How much was that worth to me? And I looked at little Skinny and told myself it was now my job to arrange for assholes to abuse her, as many as possible. The more assholes I got to fuck her, the less I would have to do. The more assholes I arranged for, the more Ancuta would be happy with me, the more food I would get, the more sleep I would have.

I could not tell you about values anymore, if I was going to be right or wrong or smart or stupid anymore. So I said, 'Okay,' and I got ready to answer the phone when it rang.

Ancuta looked at me. She said, 'Always say baby.'

'Hello,' I said, 'baby.'

We were in that apartment for three days. It was not three days of answering phones for me. It was two and half days of assholes and half a day of answering phones.

It was no problem doing the phones and it didn't make me angry or sad or crazy in any way. It was just easy to do and the assholes were so nice, so soft when they rang up and pictured the happy, fantasy girl on the other end of the telephone.

At first I felt as if I had a little piece of power in my hand, that this was something I could not just take calls with but that I could maybe, if brave enough, make calls with too.

But they did not even have to tell me that no calls could be made from these phones but 999 calls. I found that out for myself as I played with the numbers.

What would happen if I was to dial 999?

For the time being, I did not do that.

Instead, this is what the phone meant to me:

'Can I have half an hour with Layla?' they would ask.

'Yes,' I say.

'Is that Marta?'

'Yes,' I say.

'Is this Angelina?'

'Yes.'

'I want to cum in your mouth.'

'That's fine, baby.'

It is always yes, always fine.

But, as I told you, it was only three days. Because the police came again, this time the Northern Ireland police, the PSNI, the people who would answer if I called 999.

And the difference this time was that Ancuta was there when they arrived.

They knocked on the door and said nothing. Then they knocked again. And then they burst it open, smashing it back and charging in. I was in the kitchen, putting on cheap shit make-up, sitting on a chair in lingerie, and they crashed into the place like elephants.

'Stay still, stay still,' they said, 'nobody move.'

Ancuta was very quick to move into the kitchen, to vanish out of view.

A policeman brushed past me, following her, and let her into the living room. We were all gathered there as some of them went into the rooms and started looking in the drawers and cupboards. Ancuta had a phone in her hand, the same one she had been talking on moments before.

A man took out some pictures. They were the face of Ilie and the face of Vali. They had surveillance pictures of them, maybe taken in Dublin or Belfast or Romania or anywhere, I didn't know.

'Do you know these men?' they asked us, and none of us did.

'Where are your papers, your IDs?'

And we didn't know.

'All we want to know is about the men in these pictures,' he said. 'We are looking for them.'

We all shrugged, as if we did not speak any English.

They asked again, searched some more and left. They took a laptop and some phones and left us there.

'Bastards,' Ancuta said. She lifted the phone that was in her hand and began talking again. It was Ilie. She had helped him hear every word. She had another phone also, one she had pushed up her vagina so very quickly when the door had knocked.

Ilie came back with Vali in about 30 minutes.

'It's okay,' he said, 'we have another place.'

We packed up in five minutes, got into the cars and drove for five minutes. And in another five minutes we were in another apartment, this time a one-bedroom, in Custom House Square.

'It's only one bedroom,' Ancuta said. 'You must be fast with all men. Ten minutes, that's it.'

Ilie made some calls, spoke with Ancuta and Vali. He said he was disappointed, as information he had that said the new landlord might do him a good discount for sex with the girls had turned out not to be true.

'He only wants the money,' said Ilie.

Chapter Seventeen

We were like a travelling band in the weeks after that. Seven of us moved around in two cars and stopped off in different places in different cities. We ate little bits of bad food at strange hours, were abused at all hours and, all of a sudden, sometimes I would be handed a phone and told to take calls.

The girls did not speak much. No one spoke much. Ancuta shouted sometimes and gave us slaps sometimes – mostly me – but the dirty little crime business just chugged along on its own track.

Where did we go?

From Belfast, we went back to Galway, then Limerick, then Cork. We went to Dublin, to Dublin Airport, to Sligo, to Wexford, to Athlone and Bray. We went back to Belfast, then to Derry, then Donegal and then Dublin. We were 'new in town' in every town, as if those words really meant anything.

Where did we go?

I don't know. No one could know. We went to the places for a short time and then we went to other places for a short time. I could read the signs on the roads now and always knew what time it was, but still this life was cars and assholes and beds and apartments and more assholes and sometimes saying, 'Hi, baby.'

Ilie was all this time building his business in Galway, always in contact with people there about what was happening, who was doing what and how much money people were making.

He would tell his friend there that Northern Ireland was good because of the money that could be made. He said the Northern Irish pay in pounds the same figure that people in the Republic of Ireland pay in euros.

But he had met some problems there, he said; the police had been looking for him right away and he had not made all the right connections he needed with the landlords yet.

'I will be going back,' he said. 'Belfast will be good for us.'

We went to Cork once, just once. Ilie was due to meet with some other pimps there and all of them had plans for us to take a big house, five or six bedrooms, near the city centre. They were excited about it, thinking that it would be a good place for them to do business, that for a little while there would be a huge brothel where the costs were very low and where all the girls could be abused all the time in all the rooms.

The landlord spoke with the pimps as we sat in one big room in tracksuits. There was almost no furniture. Some of the walls were bare. The house looked like it had been stripped of everything. We knew there was a deal being struck, but that there seemed to be an issue. There was so much whispering, so much silence and staring and three-second phone calls by the pimps that it was hard to ever really know the detail of what they were doing.

Ilie came in and whispered to Ancuta. They looked at each other and she shrugged.

She told us to get up, to go into the hall and get the paint pots, to bring them in. Paint pots and brushes and rollers and trays.

'You are going to paint the house,' Ancuta said, 'for the landlord.'

The landlord knew what slaves were. Even more than that, he knew what sex slaves were and this suited him very well. He was going to have his fun.

Ilie said, 'Paint the walls naked.'

I don't think we were very surprised. I already knew there were a lot of people with problems with their heads, so this was just another asshole with problems.

He wanted trafficked women to work naked in his house. And he wanted to have sex with them too. All of us. I don't know what deal Ilie was getting from this, but I would think he was paying no rent at all.

When we started there were six of us, naked and painting and decorating. And Vali was setting up computers in the kitchen, lining us up for business as we painted in the living room and the bedrooms and the hallways.

Ancuta did some of the assholes as we worked, but soon she was ordering me and others to go and do the asshole who had arrived or who would be arriving in five minutes.

I didn't give a shit that I had paint on my hair or my legs, that the house stank of it. None of these things is important. But now I think how it must have seemed strange.

There were not many assholes. Most of the work was painting. All day, brush up and down, roll up and down, emulsion on the walls and gloss on the wood.

Some floors had carpet on them, and we had to cover it with plastic sheets so the paint did not splash. And then when we had finished with a room we had to take the vacuum cleaner and do the carpets.

Ilie and some of his friends, arriving from different parts of the south-west of Ireland, sat on chairs in the garden and smoked and drank, and some of his friends snorted cocaine, and we painted walls.

The landlord would come and go during the day, stand in the room and watch us as we worked. White, white, white everywhere. All the walls white. The ceilings had mostly been done, he said, but the walls needed the work. More and more paint, more and more white. Onto stepladders to paint more white.

We were there for maybe seven days. One day he called to us all, he said, 'Come upstairs,' and we were told to follow him upstairs.

He had six girls sit on his bed with him, all naked. I sat at the top, a little behind him.

When he looked at me he said, 'I want you,' and I moved back. I hated this man. He was in his fifties, stinky, horrible, strange. I couldn't have him touch me. It just came into my head that I would not let this one be near me.

'I want you,' he said and I moved off the bed.

He did it with other girls and I was there. Ancuta found out after that I had not behaved, done what he said. She grabbed me by the wrist and shook it hard.

'You stupid?'

'No.'

'Spoilt bitch.'

'No.'

She told me to brush all the wooden floors, and that was fine. I had escaped something and I hadn't escaped anything for a long time. I felt as if I still had some fight left. This was sexual slavery and labour slavery at the same time and I had broken away from at least some of that. A small victory was a big victory in my situation.

I don't know why we left that house because I thought we would be there longer, but we left when it had been painted and all the girls but me had been abused by the man.

Ancuta didn't speak with me as we drove away. I don't remember where we went. Maybe Galway again, maybe Limerick. Maybe we went to Dublin. Yes, I could see better with my glasses but it didn't matter; it was a sense that was not helping me make sense of my daily life.

Now and then, in one of our different locations, Ancuta would get drunk, drunk and drunk. She would cry and complain about her life and say she missed her little son back in Romania and drink more. Sometimes she would look at us as if she really did think we cared for her. It was crazy. Skinny would look sad when Ancuta was sad, but I can't say that I did.

I didn't cry, not too much anyway, after a while, and I think I laughed only once. And I didn't pretend at any time that I was interested in the life of Ancuta Schwarz. She can die and burn in hell for all I care, and the sooner the better.

So this one night she was crying and moaning about her life and then, of course, she got angry with the world. And a text arrived from Ilie, who was out doing something, and it made her mad. And that meant we were in trouble.

We were in the kitchen in an apartment in Dublin and she went to get more vodka. A phone was ringing and a man had been shouting at Lily in the bedroom. There was anger in the air.

Skinny, like me, was just in underwear and Ancuta was in a robe. Skinny started saying something to Ancuta, something about her getting a cold, that she had sneezed on a man and felt very low. It was something like that.

Ancuta started raging, shouting in her Bucharest lingo. She pulled a knife from the kitchen, a long blade, and was swinging it around, shouting at Skinny. I wanted to put my head down and cover my face with my hands. I felt like she was going to cut Skinny open with it. So Skinny stood up and backed towards the door with her hands out.

Ancuta was saying, 'You bitch, you fucking bitch, you don't know anything,' and moving towards her.

She slapped her hard across the face with one hand and then slapped her back again. She held the knife right up to her and Skinny tried to turn away.

Ancuta swung the knife, as if to threaten her, as if she was about to cut her face off. I could see Skinny shaking and shivering and crying.

I was on my feet, with no plan, just saying, 'Stop it, stop it.'

Ancuta swung again with the knife. I wish I could have stopped her but my only idea was to turn away.

Ancuta shouted, 'Blind bitch' and I stood there, frozen. Ancuta shouted more and then her hand, slap, slap, slapped at me, the knife in her other hand slicing at the air. She was just crazy on drink, crazy again.

The phones were ringing and Skinny was crying, I was crying, Ancuta was shouting. My hands were over my face and I wanted to pull my own eyes out or pull my own stupid head off. I felt like I was imploding with hate. It was all running through every part of me, yet only inside; on the outside I was too scared to move, to look at this devil woman.

It was moments like this she terrified me, terrified everyone. She was like a rabid dog, like some kind of woman possessed by demons. There was no reasoning with her and she was capable of anything.

Suddenly, she took the knife back into the kitchen and I watched her put it away. Why didn't I just get that thing and stick it in her face? Why did I not do that? Why am I not telling you now that I am a killer? Why am I not saying this to you from prison?

I don't know. I have no logical, honest, sensible answer. Maybe you are saying, 'Anna, go and get that same knife now and cut the bitch's throat,' but of course I didn't do that.

I'm glad now I didn't do it but if I had been a little stronger in one way, a little more crazy in the direction that she is crazy, I would have killed her on that day.

Skinny went to the chair and wiped at her tears before crawling up into a helpless little ball as she always did.

There was no reaction from Ilie when he came back a little while later.

There were three other girls there at the time, and they were like many of the girls I have met. They were drugged-up, messed-up people. If you can believe this, I felt that one of them was jealous of us. I felt she thought we were now the centre of attention for Ilie, that he would be looking out for us more now.

Chapter Eighteen

A week later and my back was sore and stinging from the cut. We had left Dublin for Galway, for another apartment in Salthill, and it was there where I met Laura for the first time.

Her pimp was also in Galway and was finding his way around. He arranged to meet with Ilie and Vali and they had heard of Laura before.

The way it worked was that a girl would be brought to Ilie and he and the pimp would see how things went. If Ilie wanted he could make an offer and the pimp would leave her with him. It is like door-to-door sales, where they let you test a product before buying. This was what Laura's pimp was doing; this was how he was seeking to make some money and begin to establish himself in the city.

Laura was from Romania. She was 35 then and her face was in a bad way. Five years before she had been forced head first into barbed wire. Pimps had beaten her and pushed her half naked into the sharp steel. Her face had been ripped to pieces. There were many scars, some long and some short. She had been in surgery because she had been cut up so badly. She was stitched all over and when the scars had healed, she went back to work for the pimps.

Laura had been away from Romania for maybe six years and had a big drug problem. Back in her home country she had a little boy, I think about eight years old, and she had not seen him in all that time. Now she was physically disfigured and mentally disfigured too, and I think so unhappy and so used to being unhappy that she did not even know. I don't think she knew what happiness was.

They used her for domination, as someone for men to slap and whip and beat. She was not on the Escort Ireland website, but was known by word of mouth. The men who liked to come and hurt the women liked to have something to shout at them, liked to be able to call them 'slut' and 'ugly bitch', something to make it easier for them to hate and hurt a stranger.

Laura was the perfect woman for this. She was skinny, someone who looked as if she had been held in a dungeon without food. Her face was a mess, she was a mess, what a seller of clothes or chocolate would say was damaged goods. Assholes sometimes do not want beauty when they want to dominate; they prefer to have something that they like to think has faults. In business terms she was, as Ilie and Vali liked to say, 'a monster'.

Her pimp was a small man, maybe only 30. I don't know his name or his story, but he had a backpack he carried with Laura's things in it. There was a whip, some chains, some hard clamps for her nipples and other tools of the trade.

I knew her only for a short time because that place in Galway was not the right place for her. Ilie said after a while that she needed a place of her own where the men could spend longer, not a place like ours where they were in and out all the time. He said she should be moved on to a place where the men could really shout and she could really scream, some cave or dungeon. The men we were with and the abuse we were taking, he said, were the normal, quiet kind. He thought of it as more respectable.

I spoke with Laura a few times, but it was like there was no one to speak with. She had, of course, a brain and a mind and a heart but all of those things had become hidden behind the hardest wall a human can have. She was probably once beautiful.

There would not be so much noise when she was being abused, only really from the assholes. Maybe Laura was so used to whatever it was they did to her that she had no sound to make about it. They would rush out of there, maybe even faster than they normally left. I think the guilt of being hateful, of adding another layer of misery onto a woman's life, would maybe get into their horrible minds. They would be leaving so very quickly to go home and kiss their wives.

But I did hear her shout a few times, a couple of screams, which maybe they had told her to do; but it was only a few days before she was gone. Do you know, if I had to make a guess, I would say that woman might no longer be alive. I would say that woman was not going to be strong enough to take much more and I think she might have, one way or another, come to her end.

There are pimps who will kill girls, you can be certain of it. Unregistered and unknown, hidden away, working like slaves, and then if they become more trouble than they are worth the easiest thing is for them to be killed. Maybe one day we will know some numbers, some more stories of those who died along the way, but the secret, online, fantasy, tucked-away nature of all of this business keeps that information untold.

If you choose to believe that I must be wrong about this, then that is up to you. But if you can account for the well-being of all the thousands of girls trafficked from Romania, from Albania, from Ukraine and other places who fall off the radar, then you are welcome to do so. A lot of mothers and fathers would like to hear from you.

I was slapped a lot by the men. They usually do it in a playful way on the bottom and then harder, then around the front, then the breasts and face. It gets harder and harder. There were times I was slapped around like a chicken breast. It did not happen too often, but it happened. Some wanted to tie my hands and there were times I just let it happen. Some wanted me to tie their hands, and I just got on with it. I have done that and slapped bottoms and dicks and balls and faces. I have watched middle-aged pot-bellied executives close their eyes in a joy and a pain as I kicked them in the balls.

I have no explanation why any of this happens any more than I have an easy explanation as to how I ended up doing it, as to how I had not killed myself or someone else up to this stage, but then this cannot be a story of explanation. There is no sensible explanation for the world I am talking about.

'Your mother,' Ancuta would say, 'is a fucking bitch who doesn't care about you.'

'Okay,' I would say.

She would pull my hair and say, 'Your mother is getting fat and isn't worried about you.'

'Whatever,' I would say.

'A pimp is going to get your mother to work in Bucharest for perverts,' she would tell me.

'That's fine,' I would say.

The threats to her and my safety, after a while, became so common that they meant nothing. That cannot have been a good thing and I was aware of that at the time, that I was becoming a little bit desensitised. I would think about that when I looked at Laura. The real difference between me and Laura was that she was no longer scared of anything at all. I was becoming resistant to it, she was already completely resistant to it. That stupid part of my brain that liked to hint to me that this was my life, that maybe Ilie was a strong man, a protector, that maybe things could have been worse, told me that Laura had reached a strange place of happiness. She was afraid of nothing. I was maybe becoming like her.

Sometimes I could judge which men were the sort who left reviews. There were no real regulars for me, and the regulars were often the ones who left very good reviews, because Ancuta did not like us to get to know anyone. And after a while we had moved around Ireland so much that there could be no regulars.

But some of them would watch your face, say things to see if you were going to smile, to see if you were 'glad' to see them, to see if your body language said to them that they were such lovely people for coming and paying to see you.

The assholes who wanted to note details like those were the ones who would go online after, onto the comments section, and say, 'Oh this one Alexa was not in a good mood when we met.'

'Oh she was not a good lover and she did not behave like a true GF (girlfriend) when I asked on the phone for the "GF experience".'

'Oh this one was not wearing make-up in a sexy way and looked really bored and didn't make eye contact.'

Ancuta hated bad reviews. 'You blind bitch, look at this,' she would say.

'Okay,' I would say.

She would slap the back of my head, eat some of her chicken/fried rice and tell me, 'You think you're too important to do this? You're a girl with a job that other girls want, you bitch.'

'Okay,' I would say.

She would munch on her food and look like she was going to spit it in my face.

And then another slap.

'Look at Skinny,' she would say, 'she is so good at the GF, the men love her. They buy her things. They buy her make-up, perfume. You don't like to be loved? No one ever love you or buy you nice things, blind one?'

'Okay,' I would say.

I had been given perfume, you know. I had been given mascara and certain colours of lipstick. I had been given sometimes knickers or some shit necklace or bangle, some little nick-nack some asshole picked up in order to prove he was a wonderful gentleman. In one case I was given chocolates, a little box of Milk Tray, and I opened them and ate many of them as the old man was pulling on his trousers.

'You like those?' he said.

'Yes,' I said.

Ancuta found the box under the bed. I had eaten the top layer, enough to make me feel sick, but up to then I had enjoyed them. She found the box and called me a greedy bitch.

'These are for sharing, greedy bitch,' she said, and took the rest for herself.

Ancuta would see everything, take everything. She would see into every corner of every room and remove anything she saw. She would sleep, over time, in every bed, sit up drunk and search through every inch of every apartment we had.

And you know she probably didn't even need to. She had her spies, her little Skinny who told her everything she asked, her Lily who shivered every time she was close.

Those girls could do the GF experience, but I could not and I did not. I did not have the strength to act as if I was delighted to see any asshole, to ever cuddle with him and call him 'baby' to his face. I did not have the actions or the smiles inside me; I was freaked out at the idea of holding hands and sharing a glass of wine. When an asshole just took his dick out and I sucked it, it was less of a lie. When he grabbed my tits and insulted me and twisted my vagina and made me sore, it was a true story. At least when he was screwing, he was close to cumming, which meant he would be out of my life soon. And every girl just wants her rapist to leave the room.

Sometimes I would be asked, 'Would you like me to leave a review?'

My answer would be, 'I don't care.'

I was asked once, 'What would you like me to say in the review? I don't want you to get in trouble.'

And I thought to myself, 'What a gentleman. You must know I am a trafficked woman, you have just screwed me and now you are trying to help me not get in trouble with my pimp.'

I hope you understand the sarcasm when I say, 'What a gentleman.'

Any man who uses trafficked women, and knows he is using trafficked women, is not a gentleman. He is a bastard.

I told the man who asked me that, 'Write what you want.'

'I'm just trying to help,' he said.

'Then go,' I said, because that was how he could help me the most.

By the time we had been to Belfast and I had started doing the phones, I was also starting to take money. I was not always escorted all the time to my room by Ancuta anymore and the men were not always escorted to the room where I was anymore.

She was showing me that she had trust in me, and I knew that if I was to mess that up then I would be beaten hard and it would be back to the start. I had been promoted in the business and was being trusted as if I was a volunteer, an employee, as if I was a willing part of the operation.

But you do not need to be willing to need trust. I know this now. You will be trustworthy if it makes your life easier and of all the things I needed in the world I needed most to make my life easier. So yes, I'm telling you that I asked for the money from clients when they walked in the room and that I took that money, left the room, gave it to Ancuta or Ilie and went back into the room and was abused.

Did I call myself a prostitute? No. Never. Would someone else? Yes, everyone. I was doing everything a prostitute does. Why wouldn't someone say I was a prostitute? Well in truth, I was a prostitute in the same way that a woman pushed out of an aeroplane is a skydiver.

But that word, prostitute, is a strange badge. It offends me but it pleased some other women. The mind gets so washed, so bleached and drugged and bumped and rewired that the word can be something to be proud of for some people. There are women who say they are happy being prostitutes and I have no quarrel with them, that is fine. I think that is okay for them and if they really mean it then good for them. If that is your life and you are sure you chose it, then fine.

And there are women, like women I have met, who take pride in being prostitutes and that is because it is the only thing they have. That job, that role of being desired and having a cash value, is all there is in their lives. And in the world where I lived, those women – trafficked women – are the ones you can trust the least. Some of them, their minds emptied, would look at me, see me bringing in this money, and they would snort their cheap cocaine and say I was the miserable 'blind bitch' who could not be trusted.

But you know no little girl grows up wanting to be a prostitute. I could never forget that I was being abused daily, that I was not a volunteer. I never fell into the easier trap of getting high as much as I could, as much as Ilie would allow, and saying, 'This is fine, this destruction of me is okay if I just think it's okay.'

Unlike many trafficked women, I was never in what they say is debt. I did not arrive having had a job promised and having had my travel paid for, only to find out that it was not the job I thought it would be. That is part of the mindset that controls these women. They tell themselves to get on with it, to be as happy as they can because, once they raise so much money for the pimps, they will be free.

That was never a hole into which I could fall, a way of keeping myself comfortable. I was maybe in more of a reality because I never really believed that this would have its own natural ending. I never made any arrangement to arrive and never discussed leaving with anyone. I never discussed what I had to make before I would again be able to walk out in my own clothes into my own life. I was never so deluded because I had arrived in a way that made it clear that I had been stolen. And what criminal ever puts back a stolen thing, when he knows it could get him into trouble?

The girls making money get a tiny share of the money they make. They are kept for unknown periods of time and if they are set free then so often they are so screwed up that they just come back to where they were. The only people they know in their new country are the people who have raped them or sold them and they have learned to handle both. Where do you go after that?

I was never in debt but this false story, this false agreement I had made with Ilie to 'work for him' and to 'make money', stayed in the background all the time. There was never a figure, never a day when I was told if I work for a certain amount of time and make a certain amount of money I will be free. It was all a lie.

Yet Ancuta was so very crazy in her head that she randomly kept telling me I owed her money. In her strange mind I ate toast and chips and whatever I could but I did not pay for it.

When she bought me that Primark robe, even though she was playing her game of being nice to me, she said, 'I added it to your bill.'

All I could say was, 'Okay.'

She would say, 'That bread was expensive, blind one, it's 30 more euros from you.'

I would shrug and go, 'That's fine.'

'Be faster with the next man,' she would say, 'because you have 100 more euros to make in this next hour because you drank whisky yesterday.'

'Okay,' I would say.

And, you know, I would say, 'Why do you not make it 1,000 euros?'

'Shut up, blind bitch.'

'Why not make it 100,000 euros and add it to my bill?'

'Shut up, blind bitch,' she would say. She would grab my hair hard and say, 'I'm going to make sure your mother is punched in the face tonight.'

'Okay,' I would say.

'Ilie says he would not even touch you now, blind bitch,' she would tell me. 'You are so filthy now, you have no care for yourself at all, you stink.'

'Okay.'

And it was true, I did stink. Of course I stank. Ancuta stank too. She would spray perfume over the smell of cum, spray it onto her body and clothes, but she stank of perfume-coated cum.

I stank even though I showered as much as I could. I hated having cum on me, having the fingerprints of those men all over me and up me.

You know, when I first arrived, I told you about the bleach. I told you that Ancuta put bleach in a soap dish and said that was all I could wash with?

Well, when I started using soap I felt as if it wasn't enough. I missed the bleach. It didn't burn but the smell was chemical, industrial, as if it was killing the poison that was being put onto and into my body. I may be the only person ever who missed washing their body with water and bleach.

I would fill the sink and pour in a splash of it, rinse my face and hands and around my neck. I would soak my hands in it. It makes the skin dry, makes it red and sore, and the smell of it is not the smell of anything that you should be putting on your body. But it kills germs, and the germs were the remains of my rapists.

Some of the girls never washed, never cared about the cum or the stink of it, about the spittle and smeg and sweat of the men on their bodies. They had just stopped sensing it, stopped telling themselves they had been violated and stopped telling themselves they had the juices of their violators stuck to them like they were a crime scene.

There were times when you could not eat because of the stench in those apartments, the stink of it all mixed together day and night and night and day in one small space. The constant cigarette-smoking masked it to some extent, but my nose, my mind would never let me lose the smell. I would notice it every day and it would sometimes make me retch.

When they showered, the girls who did not care, you knew they were probably planning to go somewhere or do something. Some of those girls would leave with Ancuta sometimes, or leave with their pimps, or leave with each other. They had a freedom to do things I could not and they saw themselves as above me for having that ability.

They would be given some cash and off they would go to buy something in a shop, which made them feel like they were succeeding and achieving in life. And they would come back and snort cocaine and discuss what was being sold in the shops and their plans to buy fur coats and take holidays in Italy and get themselves rich boyfriends, as if all of that was only a matter of time.

And they would become targets for penises again, stink after stink after stink, and they would fill their mouths with them and think about how things were getting better.

Chapter Nineteen

In September they wanted to sell me.

The first I heard of this was a conversation in a hotel room at Dublin Airport. We were moving around a lot as Ilie managed his fears about being tracked down by giant Travellers working for his enemies. And now we were at the airport and they were advertising online to people coming and going on planes that we were prized fresh meat.

My pimps made no secret of their hopes. They hadn't been too confident about my work on the phones, always feeling they had to have an ear and an eye on me, and that was not ideal for them. And I was not earning what I had been earning for them as a hooker. I had been around a long time, I had reviews under all my aliases, I was known and anyone who walked into a room and looked knew I had been abused by many men. Of course, lots didn't care, but I just looked now like a tired, bruised prostitute and not like tender, spirited, fresh meat who was full of the spirit to fight and fuck. I looked like I was not still vulnerable, that I had been someone else's vulnerable and I had lost. There is a difference in value. I did not look like I could be won.

There were bruises all the time. I bruise easily so it was as if every slap, every rape, every punishment left me marked some more. There were always old ones fading away, new ones appearing, always fresh bruises where previous bruises had been. My lower back had become weak where I was shoved and pushed and punched by passing pimps and seized and pressed by assholes. And, of course, my back had a knife scar that didn't look too pretty. My arms and legs were marked all over and my hips ached, causing me pain from my lower back right down into my legs.

My hair was thin at the back, from being pulled out by Ancuta, and it was as dry and lifeless as my skin. My whole body, slower than ever to heal, was undernourished and ugly. My eyesight was worse than it had ever been and useless without my glasses. My teeth were damaged, my breath smelled and my hearing was bad on one side.

I was their million-dollar baby but I had made my million, or whatever figure it was that I had made for them. So I was becoming baggage, taking up space in their rooms and car after I had passed my maximum earning potential.

They told each other if they cleaned me up and made it clear I had been a big winner for them in Galway, then they could get a good price for me. I didn't know what the price was and didn't care. I had been sold before for 30,000 euros and had no idea how that figure had been reached, so I had nothing to base any of this valuation stuff on. I had no idea where my life was going to take me next.

Planes were taking off and landing all the time and you could hear them in those hotels where we were abused at Dublin Airport. The pimps would book two rooms beside each other for two or three nights and one would be in constant use while everyone waited in the other room. If busy, they would split up and both rooms would be used, but mostly it was just one room at a time in each hotel. The asshole arrives at the airport on a plane or to take a plane, looks up an escort, rings up, walks over to the nearby hotel, goes to the room and does his act. No one knows anyone. It is very comfortably safe for assholes at airports. There is always a lot of business.

We would be in one or two or more hotels at a time, depending on how many girls and pimps were with us. When we were leaving, we would be leaving behind bags of used condoms for the cleaners. I am sure they must have despised us and I can't blame them.

And those planes in the air above us all the time, going all over the world, happy families and people on board from lucky countries with money in their pocket, and it would make me wonder if this was it for me, this would be my life, that the hopes and dreams I had as a little girl were just the wishful thinking of an ignorant, blind fool. So it was here that I heard I too could be moving on and there was no excitement about any possible journey.

We went back to Galway, some other apartment near the city centre, and it was from there one day that I was told to get my things.

Ancuta gave me a little flower-patterned dress that she said would fit and told me I had to pay her for it.

I said, 'Okay.'

We left Vali, Rena, Lily and Skinny behind and Ilie, Ancuta and I went to Dublin. They told me before I arrived at the airport I knew so well that we were going to Romania. This was news that shocked me to the bones.

'To sell me there?' I asked.

'We will see,' Ilie said.

If they were taking me to see the sort of people they knew in Romania, nothing good was going to happen.

Ancuta had my passport, the one Ilie had used to rent an apartment, and we boarded a plane for Bucharest. I could see many other Romanians on board and felt like I wanted to see every face. But I think people so often don't even look at other people on planes, they just get on and off and don't want to do anything that might make them have to get social.

I felt as if, among everything else, I had lost my manners, lost an understanding of how to behave. I remember looking at everyone and wondering what they did and where they were from, but never saying 'Hello' or smiling or nodding or behaving like a normal human being, never mind a lady. Maybe I was looking for a friendly face, a face from Sibiu that I could trust. To do what? I don't know. I wasn't sure if I even believed in trust anymore.

Ten people – I counted them all – came to meet us at Henri Coanda Airport in Bucharest. They were all from Roma backgrounds, some friends of Ilie and some friends of Ancuta who lived in the city.

Where I was standing, I was four hours by road from my mother. I was as close to her as I had been since before I was taken but I knew we might as well be three light years apart.

We drove to a former house of Ancuta's, on the outskirts of Bucharest, and went indoors. I was not asked anything and I did not say anything. It was here that I met some of her friends, contacts and relatives. One woman there could only twist her face up as she looked at me, and she kept looking at me. She looked at me like I was shit.

She looked disgusted and then said, 'She sucks too much cock.' They all laughed at her words.

They ate some soup and chatted about life in Ireland and about what some old friends in the area were doing. They talked about the prostitution trade without mentioning sex or abuse or rape, as if it was just talking about the business of a newspaper shop. It was very clear that money was coming from Ireland into this network, and that most people there would at some stage or other spend time in Ireland or Britain and play their part in earning money through the slave sexual labour of others.

They passed around bread and talked over all this as I sat alone, on a small sofa at the back of the kitchen, and did not eat the soup I had been given. I felt disgusting. I felt sick. I felt empty and full of hate and shame and stupidness. I would be sick if I ate anything.

Ancuta came over, told me to follow her out of the room. She took me to a different downstairs room, full of pictures and piles of what looked like junk, and we stood in front of the mirror.

'Make-up,' she said, passing her little bag to me.

And she watched as I put it on before she sprayed me down with perfume, like it was weedkiller.

Then myself, Ancuta, Ilie and a group of others got into a car and drove to some sort of crappy nightclub. She snatched the glasses from my face as we arrived. Some men, unshaven, unpleasant, were waiting at the front, smoking cigarettes. Ilie got out first and they all shook hands, patted each other on the back. He knew them from before.

He waved over and Ancuta got me out of the car and walked me over to the men as a little drizzle of rain came down. They liked what they saw and Ilie turned me around, a 360-degree spin.

'Not half a million,' laughed one of the men.

And this was the first time I had heard this number. Half a million euros. They wanted to sell me for half a million euros. This was a crazy number. What were they thinking?

'Really popular in Ireland, a real expert with real class,' said Ilie, 'and young. Can do phones, speaks English, German, everything.'

'Why are you selling?' one man said.

'It's what I do now,' he said.

They all laughed.

And that bit was true. Ilie was beginning to change the shape of his operation, to focus more on trafficking east Europeans via Ireland into Britain, into Sweden, into Germany and other places where he was making valuable contacts.

He had learned much in Belfast, learned that Northern Ireland is an easy back door into Scotland, England and Wales because it is also in the UK. Approaching Britain from Europe with trafficked women was not as simple. Bringing them to Ireland and then into Northern Ireland and over the water was easier.

It was important to him that those involved in the operation, back where it all begins in Bucharest, knew he was moving along, moving up. I believe he wanted to give them that message by way of bringing me there and pitching me at such a high value.

'No way,' the man said, 'too much.'

These men did not look rich, they did not look as if they would even have half a million euros, but looks are deceiving. This trade in human beings, in sex trafficking, is worldwide but the roots of it run especially deep in Romania. Countless thousands of euros go into Bucharest from across Europe and further, all down to the abuse of Romanian women on foreign streets by foreign assholes.

Half a million euros, in the big picture, is not too much for something that they believe will make it back for them. But, despite my skills, I do not believe that I looked like half a million euros.

I don't know if this deal would have been for the buyer to pay up front, or to pay some up front, or for Ilie just to leave me with him for a time to start earning and see how it went. All of these pimps have their own rules and ways of doings things.

The man looked me up and down again.

They discussed my body a little while more. I had a feeling that Ilie would drop the price, but the man was not keen.

I stood there, in the cold night air, waiting for them to agree on my value or call it off. And soon Ancuta, disappointed, grabbed my arm and pushed me back towards the car. I had not been sold.

'Ilie priced you much too high,' she said to me. 'He is stupid. Ridiculous.'

Ilie again shook hands with all the men and they chatted and smoked and said their goodbyes and off we went.

That night we stayed at Ancuta's old house. I stayed in a room downstairs with Ancuta, who got up early the next morning and left. It was only a few days later that she told me she had seen her son there, that she had spent an hour with him that morning. I don't know any more than that. We flew back to Dublin that day and she did not speak.

There had been texting and ringing to Ilie and Ancuta, which they learned when we touched down in Ireland. They both turned on their phones and many messages came through as we left the plane.

Vali had got drunk, made a mess of things in Galway. He had lost Skinny and Lily. They had gone, run from the apartment. Now these were not two girls who were the kind to betray their pimps, but they had been talking and had both been at a bad stage. They had both found the courage, with the domineering figures of Ancuta and Ilie gone, to do something, to stand up, to test fate, find hope and run for their lives.

'You fucking fool,' Ilie said to him, shouting into the phone. 'When did they go? What did they take? What are they wearing? Do they have a phone?'

All these questions, all because he was going to get this fixed as fast as possible.

'Check the bus station and train station in Galway and we will do the same here,' he said.

His thinking was that the girls had nowhere to go. They could run all they wanted in Ireland, but two bruised Romanian hookers on the run from pimps are not exactly welcome everywhere. They are at the top of no lists when it comes to ideal surprise visitors. Their real options were, one, the police and, two, the airport.

The police would be told that these two convicted prostitutes had run from a brothel. They would right away want to know details of who ran the brothel because that's where the law comes in, that is the interest of the police. Like very many Romanians, experience and word of mouth told them always to be wary of the police, to not trust them too much. And experience in Ireland told them that going to the police as trafficked women would not necessarily have a good outcome.

I cannot see that the two girls would have wanted right away to get into more trouble with Ilie. The two girls, you see, who agreed to come to Ireland to 'work on webcams', who agreed to work for Ilie, would want only to get out of the country. These are two girls with broken English who had no proof Ilie ever did anything to them, who had no evidence about Ancuta ever harming a hair on their heads. Would these two confused, abused, scared girls with families in danger back home have the attitude and mindset to get into all of that?

I didn't think so.

Their other serious option was just to go home. To try to make it to the airport, to try to get a plane back to the land of their birth, to find friends who would help them and to try to restart, or at least take time to take stock of, their lives in Romania.

In truth, neither option was promising, but the second one, even though there was of course risk to their loved ones, was better than the first.

And if I was thinking this, Ilie would also be thinking this. He knew the minds of his girls. He knew the thoughts of scared and lonely people because he created scared and lonely people all the time.

He looked up flight times, bus times, train times on his phone and chose his next move.

We did not have far to go. There is a bus stand at Dublin Airport where the bus from Galway arrives. We parked up close by and Ilie went to watch. He checked the time and we waited. Very little was said, and we waited, in a light rain, for the night to come. And we waited. All the time it was as if he was expecting, not hoping for, his girls to appear.

And there they were, like two timid little dogs, climbing off a newly arrived bus with the little, silly, stupid hopes of getting a plane back to a place where arms would be outstretched for them and they would be safe for evermore.

I have to tell you that they did not even have their passports.

Ilie walked to them as they stepped off, each with a little bag, and they stood in front of him, nodding their heads as he spoke, immediately as obedient as ever. He walked them back to the car. They got into the back with me and we all drove back to Galway.

We all knew what would happen later.

Chapter Twenty

Ilie talked more about selling girls. He spoke to people on his phone, to the girls, to Vali and Ancuta to say he would be travelling more to increase his new line of work.

Here was this man, the man in the picture when the PSNI came crashing into our first Belfast apartment, planning lots of flights from city to city to city. It was as if he was being chased by police, but only once in a while. Did they not know he lived like a rich and free man? Did they care?

Ilie came to learn from his contacts that the best deals could be made in the Middle East. Pale, white girls were being traded in Saudi Arabia for huge sums, he believed.

In Bucharest, he discovered, there were people who could arrange for visas, fake ones, which would allow access to Saudi Arabia. His friends in London were telling him the visas had never had any problems. They were coming from the same organised gang his people had links with, gangs controlling prostitution, begging and drugs on the streets of many countries. Ilie may have had enemies in this large network but it was still possible for him to buy visas from their members in London.

It was at this time, for the first time, that I heard him speak openly about girls disappearing in the Emirates. He and Vali talked about how girls can sometimes be sold there with the condition that they are not sought again, that they are already off the grid, that no one is looking for them or will come looking for them.

It was not directly all of this that led me to change my mind. It was partly all of this, but I believe I was going to change my mind anyway. I believe I had to, that in order to turn this around to eventually start to change my life, to fix my destroyed life, I had to begin to play a game.

No hero was going to come crashing in to save me, to take me away and protect myself and my mother forever. No Liam Neeson was tracking me down, arming himself and getting ready to end the lives of Ilie Ionut and Ancuta Schwarz and all of their people. No mysterious ex-boyfriend, I considered, was going to once again appear and fix my problem and tell me to be brave forever. I would have to do this myself. I would have to think properly and begin to change things. If my life continued like this, it was not my life; it was a living death.

It was September 2011, six months after I had been stolen by these people, when I decided I would completely and fully cooperate with them at all times. I decided I would win their trust. I decided I would work for them, no longer against them, and day by day I would remove any concerns they had and make their lives easier.

Such a move would raise my value as a member of their team and give me more space, more time, more options, more chances of making a plan. Something inside me told me if I was taken to the Middle East I would never be seen again.

I told Ancuta I liked doing the phones.

'My English is the best,' I said, 'I think maybe you should remember that.'

She said she didn't like me doing the phones, she didn't like my manner, my attitude, my face when I answered the calls.

'I will change that,' I said.

She didn't trust me at all, but I was offering to help. If it didn't work out, she could always just belt me around the head a few times.

And so I really did go for it.

'Hi, baby,' I would say, chuckling, 'please come see me soon.'

'Oh hello, dear, I hope you like beautiful, sexy girls.'

'Hi, honey, are you as horny as I am? If you could see me now I am licking my lips.'

Ilie loved it. He loved it to the point that Ancuta felt she was being trumped, that he was finding himself a better professional to work the phones. But what really mattered was that, if he was liking it, then I would be kept doing it. And it was some relief to think that the more I did this work, the less I would be raped.

Soon I was in charge of five phones. I would get a sandwich and sit with all my mobiles, taking calls about all the profiles.

The phones sat on the table in front of me and I kept them on silent. No texts, no kept messages, nothing but voice calls. There must be as little trace as possible. This is just the way you do things when you are a criminal.

I still had to earn, of course, it was not so easy to get away from that. But I was more able to steer things away from me at that stage, and away from Skinny too. We were better friends than before and I think maybe we were reaching a point where she would not run to tell tales on me now if I was doing something Ilie or Ancuta might not like.

'You want me to give you fewer assholes to deal with?' I asked her.

She nodded. 'Yes.'

'Okay,' I said, 'don't you say, okay? Don't say to anyone.'

And I would tell Rena she had another man coming, I would tell Lily she had another man coming, I would tell Ancuta a man was coming who fell in love after seeing her picture.

I had it ticking over in a way that was not driving me insane every minute, and I was just about getting away with it with everyone. And then I would get the slap on the back of the head.

'You're not fucking enough today,' Ancuta would say.

'Okay,' I would say, 'I'm sorry, Cami,' the name her closest friends would use.

And I would meet more assholes.

One day, in the middle of all this, Ancuta told me there was a problem.

'You and Skinny,' she said, 'need to do a lot today.'

How much?

4,400 euros. A specific number.

One day.

Either there was an emergency for the money or she was playing very hard games with our heads. But there was nothing we could do. She paid to put up more profiles on Escort Ireland, lined up more assholes on the phones and sent them to us.

If each day was hell, then this was the centre of hell. If each day was pain, then this was the place where pain is made.

I remember it was in Belfast. It was one of the days we were back in that city and Ilie was making his connections and making his plans. He wanted to buy things, cars, jewellery, clothes, whatever. Maybe that was what we did it for. Maybe on that day we paid for the blue BMW he bought in Belfast. I don't know.

I knew he had made a good connection with a landlord who owned lots of places, a man who wanted no sexual services. The man could help him with his need for places to put his girls, but he had to be paid in cash only. Maybe that was why Skinny and I suffered that day. Whatever it was, it was someone's decision about the price of something that led to Ilie simply thinking, 'No problem.' And he would have told Ancuta, very simply, that we needed to make more.

I'm not counting for you. I have not counted and I do not want to know. I cannot remember. But myself and little Skinny were both unable to walk, unfit to stand. I don't know if I was crying or sleeping or bleeding or dying after all of that. It was inhuman.

The sums that were being transferred weekly to his people in Bucharest were a regular amount. He would not want to take in less in any one week when he bought something.

Ancuta flip-flopped to me all that day to say, 'Work harder, more, more.'

She told me to answer phones but fuck more, more, more.

She said, 'No food today, quick just fucking.'

And when she found me getting some bread and butter as I answered calls, she said, 'It's going on your bill. More debt. Work more, more, more. Don't eat.'

I said, 'Put it onto the bill. Put more onto the bill, Cami. More, more. Add up more. My big bill, make it bigger.'

She slapped me, told me I was 'filth' and 'blind' and that my mother knew I was 'screwing all the men in Ireland'.

That kind of thing was routine for her, the insults, the words she thought would hurt me, the random sums of money she said I owed.

'You owe me 9,000 euros,' she would say sometimes, or, 'You owe me 10,000 euros and when will you pay?'

'I owe you 10,000?' I would say. 'Can I make it 20,000? Or please make it 100,000?'

The only thing I owed her was misery.

'You cannot have any more food,' she said.

'Then why don't you kill me?'

'I will kill you.'

'I want you to kill me.'

'Shut up, blind bitch. Your mother will be in trouble tonight because of you.'

And she would strike me, a palm across the face, a tug of the hair, a punch on the lower back.

It became habit, her violence, to the point that I had absolutely no fear of it and barely felt any pain. I knew the little twist of her face, of her lip, that happened just before she lifted her hand. I knew when her eyes narrowed she was going to reach out, to grab me.

She would strike me, then fix her hair, wriggle her toes to straighten her flip-flops and make herself all correct and into a beautiful lady again. She would grab my hair and pull her face close to mine and tell me I was blind.

I wanted to tell her I was not blind enough to know she was an ugly bitch, inside and out, but I knew that would have been too far. She would have killed me. I spoke back to her, but I never told Ancuta she was ugly. And I never hit her.

I remember in Galway, in the second place we stayed, when there was a birthday party for Ancuta. Pimps and Mother Pimps from around the city and prostitutes and others came to celebrate. I did not know her so well then and I remember clearly thinking that I was astounded at how much she thought of herself and how little she thought of everyone else.

I sat on the sofa between men who sometimes grabbed at my thighs and vagina and breasts, and she talked to person after person and, each time, turned away and called them pigs or bastards under her breath. She hated everyone in that room, maybe even herself. She looked at me that night, when she was drunk, and told me Ilie loved her. I didn't react. Ilie came behind her and smiled at me, hugged Ancuta.

And right away she blew up at him, called me a bitch and said he must be as blind as I was if he liked me, if he was going around smiling at me like that. He said he did not like me. Ancuta slapped my head. Ilie lost his footing and fell beside me. He stood up and as he did he reached out and punched at my stomach as I sat, as if to show her he really did not give a shit about me.

Other people came over, mostly high and drunk, and told them to calm down, offered them drinks and said this was 'a party'. They said they already knew I was a filthy blind bitch from Sibiu and to not let me get between them.

Later on Ilie hit me more times, slapping me as I came into the room. He was drunk, almost falling onto the floor again, and he belted me around the face.

He was going crazy, saying to Ancuta, 'You know, Cami, this bitch is better than you.'

And she yelled at him, rage from deep inside.

'I will fuck her,' said Ilie. 'You watch and I will fuck her in front of you.'

Ancuta told me to go and sit down, and slapped me on the head and punched me in the lower back as I did.

Ilie said to her, 'You would die for money, wouldn't you? You and your son would die for money from my hands.'

And the boy he was speaking about was his own boy, their own young son back in Romania.

That was maybe the worst I had ever seen him, the drunkest I had ever seen him. And it was the worst I had ever seen Ancuta.

And yet she came to me later, all smiles, squeezed my hand and said, 'You will be fine.'

We were going to Belfast more and more as Ilie became happier about his connections. Not only was he firming up international links, but he felt he was really muscling in on the trade in the city. He believed the sex business was underdeveloped in Belfast and saw himself as becoming a big player with skills and know-how at his fingertips.

But still, from time to time we would drive the straight, quick road to Dublin Airport and check into hotels and advertise fresh meat for sale.

Sometimes we went back into the city too, particularly if there was something on, if there was a big sports match or concert and the place would be packed with drinking visitors.

The hotels – from the city centre to the quay, to the airport in north Dublin and the upmarket areas in the south of the city – knew who we were. They can spot a group like us straight away. There was a time they used to object, to warn about renting time in the room to sell sex being illegal, but that died out long ago. There was nothing they could say, not anymore. And anyway, for them we were business.

The next time we returned to Belfast it was to the richer end of the city, to the south, to the Malone Road area. We were based first in a hotel there and then on to an apartment at Windsor Park, which Ilie said would be good for business. I know my papers were used to rent the place and a form was signed, not by me, to secure the deal.

Vali and Ilie talked over the profiles and more pictures were taken, more profiles were uploaded, more and more girls made out of six girls who were there at that time. Ilie told me I would be doing more on the phones, that there would be more calls than ever and that he didn't want to lose anyone.

'Answer all the calls,' he said, 'baby, baby, baby,' adding Ancuta would be doing the same.

Lily, who I told you about, was like everyone else who wanted nothing more in this world than to get away from that business. But she told me she wanted more men, as many as she could get, to help her pay off the debts she owed to Ancuta and Ilie.

'Get me more,' she said quietly.

She believed, if she hit a target, she would soon be free to walk away and into her own life in Ireland or Britain. I am not someone who is sure it can ever work as simply as that. But I will tell you that I said, 'Okay, no problem.'

Another woman, Ella, was there at the time, arriving with another pimp. She too wanted more.

'Get me all the men,' she said.

But with Skinny it was different. Every time she was abused she felt abused, every time she was booked she was booked to be raped. A lot of the assholes liked her because she looked so young, so frail and thin and weak, because she was like a helpless child. And many times she was abused over and over by assholes who were paedophiles, fantasising that she was a little girl with no choice but to submit to them.

I spoke with her again about her work and, very quietly, we agreed that now I was doing the phones more I would steer the men away from her but that it would not always be easy. And as for me, I too was planning to be abused as little as possible.

Soon Ilie was impressed, showing yet more faith in me, asking if I needed some nice shoes, some nice new underwear, because of my phone manner. I was seeing fewer assholes and it felt as if I was achieving something, as if I was starting to disconnect from the worst of it all. In a few days, I had 16 phones, all placed down in front of me by Ilie, all the numbers advertised online.

I wondered if there were possibilities here, ways of finding out valuable information that could at some stage in the future protect me, protect my mother. I wondered at what stage, in the mind of Ilie if not Ancuta, I would become someone who should have some freedom, some money, some of her own identity back.

And the calls kept coming.

'I want to have 30 minutes with Lucy,' they would say.

'Oh she's so pretty,' I would say.

'Oh yes,' they would say, 'she's a model.'

'It's no problem, baby.'

And always, 'I want to book skinny little Lola for one hour tonight.'

'Oh, she's not here tonight, baby, but you know there is her best friend who is the same age and really wants to meet someone later.'

'Yes, that's fine.'

Then, one day, an unusual call.

A man called and told me he had rung in a few times before.

'I want,' he said, 'to book Melanie and Sabrina and Reka and Izabela and Yasmin and Alice.'

Now some of these girls were the same person, so that was not possible, but I could not tell him that.

So I said, 'Okay, baby, that's maybe not possible as they are busy girls.'

And, you know, I felt he was testing me.

'What about Eva and Mya and Coco?' he said, who were all the same person.

'Well, baby,' I said, 'can you just tell me how many girls you want?'

He waited for a moment and then laughed.

'It's okay,' he said, 'I didn't think they'd all be available at the same time.'

'Okay, honey,' I said.

He said, 'Maybe I can meet with you?'

'Oh, thanks, baby,' I said, 'I am very busy but I know—'

'Come on now,' he said, 'why can't I book you? What about for an afternoon?'

An afternoon? That was something I had never done before. I had been to hotels, but not an out-call, and I had never spent an afternoon with anyone.

'An afternoon?'

The man said, 'Yes. Four to five hours. Can you come to my place?'

Ancuta could see I was talking to one man for longer than normal. I told her when she asked. I said this man wanted to book me for the afternoon.

She took the phone and said, 'She is my best girl. I can't give her away all afternoon.'

The man said he would pay £1,000 for up to five hours on that same day.

So Ancuta said, 'That's fine, baby. I will bring her to you.'

It was the beginning of the end.

Chapter Twenty-One

We left the phones to Lily and Ella, and Ancuta asked Vali for his car keys. She asked me to drive, which was something I had not done in many months.

She gave directions from her phone and we ended up in Belfast's Cathedral Quarter. It is an up-and-coming part of the city, with lots of new apartments and shops, cafés and restaurants. Ancuta liked the idea of a client living there, someone who might have a lot of cash.

'You know who this asshole is?' she asked me, as I parked up on the street across from the apartments.

'No.'

'He better have £1,000.'

We walked through a courtyard and to the main outer door. She pressed the buzzer and he let us in. We took the lift up to his floor, walked to his door and Ancuta knocked.

'Hello, baby,' she said, smiling, 'this is Natalia.'

'You're the one I was speaking to?' he asked.

'Yes.'

He nodded.

'That's grand,' he said.

Ancuta said she would wait outside and I shrugged. She looked at the man and nodded her head.

'Four, maybe five hours,' she said.

'Yes,' he said, went back into the apartment, returned and handed over the cash.

She checked through, looked happy, turned and walked away, tucking her beloved money into her pocket.

'Come in,' he said.

The man was in his thirties and said his name was Andy. He was ordinary-looking, a Northern Ireland man with short, dark hair and a boyish face. He was wearing jeans and a T-shirt. He wore no shoes and didn't look rich.

We walked into a living room and four other men were sitting there, waiting for me to come through the door. My sunken heart sank more. This was what it would be. Five men, all afternoon. They could not get five girls, so instead they are going to punish me by just getting one girl and making her do it with five men for four hours.

My head was down but I was not scared. It would be whatever it was going to be. Whatever it was, it probably would not kill me. I hoped not anyway.

Andy walked around me, looking at my clothes. I had a hoodie on over a little top and wore a miniskirt below. I think I looked like a standard sex worker.

He started to take off my hoodie, looking at it, feeling around inside it. The others watched. He looked at them and they all shrugged.

Andy looked back to me and said, 'Take your clothes off.'

I took off my top and skirt and then my underwear and stood where I was.

The men looked me up and down, and up and down.

'Shit,' said one.

'What the fuck happened to you?' said another.

At first I was confused by this, but then I saw it their way. I was covered in bruises. My skin was all sorts of colours, from my thighs to my breasts to my neck. Some bruises had been there for a long time, some came and went quickly. I had no idea of how bad it might have been, what my current state was, because I was so used to being hit and hurt and squeezed and slapped that there was nothing to look for in my mind; I had nothing to keep count of because the bruises just kept appearing and disappearing and reappearing. Here we were in a bright room, the sun filling every inch of the place through big windows, and they could see clearly every inch of me.

'You're seriously fucking trafficked,' said Andy, 'aren't you?'

I shrugged and said, 'What do you want?'

'Nothing,' he said. 'Just checking. We're paranoid.'

The others laughed.

I didn't know what he meant.

He searched through my clothes, then handed them back.

'Put them back on,' he said.

I was surprised, maybe even shocked. I was expecting anything and everything to happen but I was not expecting that. They all watched as I dressed in front of them. It was not something I was used to doing.

'You answer like nine or ten different phones,' said Andy.

'What do you want?'

'Just to talk,' he said.

I didn't speak.

'It's not your business, right? You work for pimps?'

'It's not my business, no,' I said.

'You are their business and they treat you like that?' he said, pointing at me, at my body, my red hands, wrists.

I shrugged.

'You not want to leave them?'

They were all watching, waiting for me to start telling them things.

'You can talk,' he said, 'it's just between us. We're interested in the business, that's all.'

'I don't leave them,' I said, meaning I was so far unable to leave them, not that I didn't want to leave them, but I was leaving it open to interpretation. I still wasn't sure what was going on here.

'You don't want to leave them?' he said.

I looked at him, at them all.

They let the silence stay there. Someone had to say something. All of them were looking at me. So I said something.

'You think I want to stay with them?' I said. 'You think I want to be standing here in front of you?'

And he nodded, they all nodded. Of course I didn't want to stay with them. With a moment's thought about the situation it was totally obvious. No girl in her right mind would want to walk into this room with five unknown men waiting inside and be under orders to do whatever they said. No one in the world, if they are in possession of a brain, would want that.

'We've been looking at your business because we have a friend who is in the same business,' Andy said.

And I could not give a shit about his friend's business. I could not give a shit about what they wanted. I felt only trouble could come from this.

But I wasn't doing the talking.

So Andy told me about his friend, that he had two girls working for him and that they had not been trafficked, but that he had been hearing a lot about trafficked women in Belfast. He said his friend had been unable to bring in many clients and they had learned, from phoning around different businesses and booking escorts, that there were ways of building trade. They said they were sure I had answered the phone as a girl from lots of different countries and that I had played an organisational role in developing business for my pimps.

I was shocked by all of this. It was like they might be asking me for business advice.

'We had to check if you were wearing any kind of wire,' he said. 'We speak freely about all sorts of stuff in here.'

At first I had thought he had some kind of malformation on one of his ankles, but then I could see more clearly and realised it was a tag, a plastic, electronic criminal tag, one of those things put on people who have been to court, who might still go to prison.

'Do you know who we are?' he asked me.

'I have no clue and I don't care,' I said.

He asked me to sit down. A couple of the men got up, went to the kitchen, lit cigarettes, gave me one. I took it. Andy came closer.

'You can talk to us in secret,' he said, 'and if you help us we can help you.'

'How can I help you? What do I know? I don't know anything.'

'You know more than you think,' he said. 'You know who's who and who's doing what and how they are doing it. And, by looking at your body, I reckon you don't owe them any favours. And it looks to me like you could do with a wee bit of help.'

I shrugged again.

He said, 'What I'm saying is that this is our neck of the woods. We have business interests here and we are interested in your business and what it is doing right where we are, you understand?'

'No.'

'Look,' he said, 'you should open up with me. We are kind of dangerous people, do you understand that? We don't have a problem with you but we might have a problem with people you know.'

'Fine,' and that sounded like stupid macho rubbish to me.

'Okay.' He laughed. He said, 'Okay, you're a tough girl, I understand that.'

There was more silence.

'You know,' I said, 'the people you are talking about would not say this is your town, you understand? They would say they have a patch here now when it comes to this business. They are doing lots of business here and they are making connections with many people so maybe it's like their town too. Maybe as much as it's your town. Maybe you have to share your town some more.'

Where that came from, I don't know. But it was like sending a bullet to these men. It was like setting off a bomb. Two or three of them were looking at me as if I had said something terrible. All I had said was that Ilie was making this city a base for himself and he was doing well at it. I didn't mean it any harder than that, but I suppose it sounded like I was trying to annoy him. His manly crap did not impress me. It was not his town anyway; every town has many criminals, many people who think it is their town. I had heard enough men talk enough shit for a lifetime. Maybe subconsciously I had been telling him to put a sock in his mouth.

Andy sat back. He said, 'Well, that's an interesting way to look at it.'

I shrugged.

'That's what they say,' I said. 'They say it's their town for running girls, that they will be running more than anyone here.'

He nodded and smiled.

'They do business all over Ireland,' I said. 'These are people with a lot of friends.'

He said, 'So are we.'

I shrugged.

He said he liked the 'trick' with all the profiles, the same girl featuring under so many different names, different nationalities.

'What else did they teach you?' he said.

'Nothing,' I said. 'I don't do any of that.'

Someone brought some cocaine from the kitchen and it was offered around. I said no. I always said no. I didn't like it. I didn't like this situation at all and wasn't about to party.

After they all did a line – not their first of the day – their conversation speeded up, became more stupid. He said his friend was running what they liked to think was a 'high-end' trade, getting men to pay for beautifully dressed women who offered services. I think he was maybe trying to tell me there is a nice kind of prostitution, which is fine. I don't care about his views on that. I don't care about your views on that matter.

I told him I had no advice for him. I said I was sitting around very often with toothache and sometimes blood in my mouth. I said my body hurt all the time and that I did not wear beautiful clothes. I said I was used to getting punched in the vagina and spat on and slapped on the back of the head. I said my hair was thin at the back because it was being pulled so much.

'You think I know lots about business?' I said. 'I am the product for sale in this, not the manager.'

They didn't know where to go with that. For a time I was asked to wait in a different room as they had a conversation. It had a nice view but that wasn't what I remember most about it. There was a bag in that room, a bag with cash in it. I saw it very clearly, just against a side wall. It was like a small gym bag, the sort of thing that is easy to carry. I could see cash in the top of it. I have no idea how much was in there but it was a lot.

Was this a trap? Was there a camera in that room or an alarm on that bag? Or had they forgotten about it, not thought about it when they put me in there?

I didn't go near it. So much about that place felt strange, worrying, confusing, that I was looking forward to leaving. I was not looking forward to seeing Ancuta again, of course not, but yet I wanted them to say, 'Thanks, Natalia, you can leave now.'

It's like when they say 'better the devil you know'. This is the mindset, when your way of thinking changes, when you are more fearful of the unknown new than you are of the fear you are used to. It was why I 'wanted' to go back to my place of slavery when I was not in my most familiar surroundings.

You know, I can tell you of the times when I had opportunities, possible little chances to escape, to arrange to spend time with men away from Ancuta and Ilie, and break free from there. I can tell you too of the times when the emotion of starting to do such a thing became too much. I felt at times, just thinking about trying to escape, that I was filling up with ideas about the kind of anger my captors would have. I felt I would just fall apart if I did break free, that it would be so useless to leave one fear to dive into a sea of more fear. I can tell you these things, I can give you examples of these things, but I cannot explain them, I cannot make them make sense.

Andy spoke to me again, close up. He said, into my face, that I didn't have to suffer.

'I don't like this stuff,' he said, pointing at my body, at the bruises. 'We don't do that here and you don't have to put up with that from anyone here. Okay?'

I shrugged. What was I to do?

'If you want to work with us, with our friend, then that's okay,' he said.

It was probably a kind thing for him to say, but I don't think he understood my situation. And anyway, he was high and was saying the first thing that came into his head. I didn't say anything to him, just maybe nodded a little.

'We're always here if you need us anyway,' he said.

'Okay,' I said, 'thank you. Do you deal drugs?'

He laughed. 'No comment,' he said.

'Okay,' I said. 'What is the thing on your leg? A tag from the police?'

'Yeah,' he said, 'I was a bad boy. I have to be home at midnight every night. Isn't that terrible?'

'For dealing drugs?'

He smiled. 'I couldn't say.'

Three and a half hours had passed. It had been the strangest afternoon. I was being offered help by drug dealers, I was being asked to help drug dealers. How had I ended up in this situation?

But there was no sex, zero abuse.

I left and Ancuta was waiting in the car, the window down, smoking a cigarette.

She directed me to the driver's seat and said, 'So?'

And I told her it was fine.

I was just a little bit worried she might be told what had happened in there, about what I had said, but my instinct told me it would be kept secret.

There were bags of shopping in the car. Ancuta had been enjoying herself with £1,000.

Chapter Twenty-Two

We spent some time in Dublin and Galway. Ilie had more deals under way and wanted to put more girls onto the circuit in Belfast, to run them from his brothel there, to open another, and another after that. He wanted more people involved and to make sure it was him who would get a cut from everyone who made money there.

In Galway, when we first arrived back, we stopped off at the flat above the bookies. It was still being used; a relative of Ilie's was running it and his partner was Mother Pimp there now.

Skinny and I did not go in. I had no interest in doing so. If it had been an old house, a former place, where I had chosen to live, it might have been different, but it was a place without a single good memory. I felt it would be bad luck to even go through the door. If I had done, if I had walked in and walked up the stairs and walked into that living room, I would have been just one of those girls, one of those many girls who stopped by with a passing pimp, like all those who did when I was living in that place. I might have seen some girl trying to hide away in the corner and, as had happened to me, I would probably have ignored her.

Skinny and I sat in the car as Ancuta told us more about her son in Romania, about how he was the prettiest boy in the world and she hoped to make sure he had a good life, how she was going to see him again soon.

We went to another place, where Skinny and I were given a bedroom. A profile was changed and phones started ringing and assholes began arriving.

'You are beautiful,' the men said.

'Okay,' I said.

'Can I cum on your face?'

'Okay.'

'Will you finger my ass?'

'Okay.'

'I love you.'

'Okay.'

It was maybe four weeks and we were back in Belfast again, back at Windsor Park. Vali had been there all the time and seemed satisfied with things. Some other girls and pimps had been and gone. There were some girls there at the time who I had never seen before. Or maybe I had seen them and couldn't remember. It became like that. There were no friends, no long-lost pals. It was just people wading through shit and passing by each other.

I took to the phones again, directing the stupid traffic once more, the horrible people calling at all times of the day looking for their dreams to come true.

Andy phoned again.

'Hi, Natalia,' he said, and he could have said any name.

'Hi, baby,' I said.

'It's Andy here again,' he said, a chuckle in his voice.

'Oh hi, Andy.'

'Can we book you for the afternoon?'

'Why?'

'Because we want to chat with you a bit more, is that okay?'

'I don't know. I think maybe—'

'You've been away and now you're back. I can tell by watching the website, you know.'

'What do you want from me?'

'Just to talk. Same as last time.'

Ancuta was not happy with this conversation. I looked at her, explained how the same man wanted to book me for the afternoon again. She shook her head. She didn't like this. She didn't like things getting personal, didn't like the idea of a girl with the same man for too many hours.

Her feet slapped as she walked over and took the phone. 'I have other girls.'

'No,' he said, 'I want Natalia. Same deal. Send her round.'

'Why only Natalia? You don't like other girls?'

'Are you going to send her round?'

'No, she is doing my phones,' she said. 'I need Natalia here.'

'And I need her here,' he said.

What was I to do?

Ancuta said 'No' and put down the phone. Her brain was rolling it around as she stood there. She was obviously thinking, 'What would one man want with one girl for so many hours? How much conversation would they have? Was he police or someone who was falling for her too much? Was he asking too many questions?'

Her Mother Pimp instinct told her something was different here.

But Andy was insistent. A friend drove him to our apartment. He buzzed up and was buzzed in. He knocked the door and pushed forward when it opened.

'I've come to get Natalia for the afternoon,' he said.

Ancuta was stunned, horrified.

'I said no, no, no to you on the telephone!'

We could all see Andy was high, maybe drunk, but he was pushy and determined and headstrong.

'She's coming with me,' he said, 'problem?'

He looked around, looking for anyone who was going to stop him. Ilie and Vali were not there. I don't know what they would have done if they had been.

'Why do you want her?' asked Ancuta.

He turned to her, looked her square in the face, held his two fists up as if he was riding a motorbike, stuck his crotch out and pulled his fists towards himself.

'Because,' he said, 'I LIKE TO FUCK HER!'

He was laughing then, maybe crazed on cocaine.

Ancuta had not been spoken to like this in a long time.

'All afternoon?'

'Yes.'

And then he added, 'There's five of us right, is that okay?'

A penny dropped.

'Ah yes,' said Ancuta, 'five.'

'Yes,' he said, 'we're all going to fuck her.'

'Okay,' Ancuta said and nodded at me, 'five.'

He took the cash out of his pocket and she took it from his hand right away.

He took me, in no make-up, a T-shirt and jogging bottoms, downstairs and to the car. The driver was one of the men I had met before. He took us to the flat. Some of the same men were there as before. There was also a woman,

Andy's girlfriend, and she shook hands, saying she had heard about me.

There was no immediate questioning this time, no stripping or trying to work me out. It was as if I had been taken straight into some kind of social gathering, maybe even a little party.

I was given a bottle of beer and Andy asked where had I been, what had been going on, how were Ilie and Ancuta? I had very little to say. I was so confused.

A man came over and Andy introduced him. He said I looked good and I said, 'Okay.'

He said, 'Do they threaten your family?'

I nodded, 'Yes, my mother.'

'That happens a lot,' Andy said. He nodded to his friend and said, 'If you work with this guy and give him a cut of what you earn, it would be easier for you. No threats, no beatings.'

'Okay,' I said. And again I wanted to shout to the rooftops that I wanted to stop being for sale for sex.

Andy's girlfriend wanted to talk. She was nice, so friendly. She was interested in my situation but I could not say much to her. And she understood that.

'What happened?' she said, just wanting me to give her an idea of how I got into this mess in the first place.

'They took me,' I said. 'They targeted me and took me because they could.'

'Jesus Christ,' she said. 'Why the hell are you still with them?'

I shrugged. It was the most sensible, straightforward question of them all and it was one I could not answer. I could not answer it in one go. I could not answer it in one minute or one hour. Maybe I answer it in this story I am telling you, and that is for you to decide, but it is a question exploring fear and danger and threat and risk and comfort and control and habit and deprivation and the answer is long and seems to have no sense. Like a stupid battered wife, like a stupid prisoner who keeps getting locked up again, I had somehow managed to live for nine months in a hundred places I had never wanted to be. So I had to answer her, why the hell was I still there. I was embarrassed, silent, ashamed, stuck for words.

'Because I'm afraid,' I said.

And she put her arms round me.

I didn't cry.

Later, Ancuta watched me walking, looked at my body language, my body, just to see if she could spot how much of a toll the afternoon had taken on me.

More than three hours with five men – she would have a professional interest in knowing if I could do that sort of thing two or more times in a day. But again there had been no sex. I had been to a party with some people I knew I could like. It was insane.

I heard nothing more from Andy in the following days, just more bullshit from Ilie about how he was going to earn even more money. A good deal of cash was, as ever, being sent back to Romania and that seemed to be raising his status among the leaders of the gang he was associated with. And he had been to Sweden, had met some guys, was firming up links in Stockholm and felt he had a safe trafficking route all planned. He was so pleased with himself it was disgusting.

Ancuta was drinking a lot, pissing him off, pissing everyone off, and screwing up some of the bookings on the telephones. She was talking about herself more and more and telling me all the time that she needed to go and live in Italy, in the most beautiful parts of it, and spend her life in designer swimsuits beside the pool.

When she realised I had diverted a customer from Skinny to another girl, she shouted at me. A slap came from nowhere and almost knocked me off my seat. She had a drink in one hand and, even though she hit me so hard, she didn't spill a drop. She grabbed my hair as I stood up, yanked it at the back.

'Fucking blind bitch,' she said, 'no one can trust a blind bitch from Sibiu.'

She told me she had been calling my mother and laughed about it. She said she had rung her a few times when she had drunk too much, because it was so much fun. I waved her away, went back to the phones.

A day later and, drunk again, she walked up to me while talking on the phone.

She came close and said, 'Yes Anna, your daughter Anna is still fucking all the men in Ireland. She is fucking one right now.'

I didn't believe what she was doing, more bullshit from this bullshit woman. But when I heard just a tiny piece of a word, a very small bit of sound from the phone she had to her ear, I knew it was my mother.

I gasped.

Here was the woman who brought me into this world, here was I making what I had so far made of it, on the phone to a man who wanted to pay for sex. I was silent. I had nothing to say to her, to the man, to anyone. I was afraid. I did not want to talk to my mother. Perhaps I did not want her to know I could be doing such a thing in such a place.

Ancuta ended the call, smiled, slapped me as hard as she could. She shouted, 'You think I'm lying to you about your bitch mother?! I LOVE to call your mother and tell her about her blind bitch!'

She was roaring to the point that Lily came into the kitchen to go, 'Ssssshhhhh!' Our precious clients would have been able to hear what was going on.

Ancuta whispered, 'We have an invitation for you to work in Dubai, Anna. You will be going out there and you can cry for your mother all you want, blind bitch.'

Tears were welling in my eyes. Phones were buzzing. Assholes were wanting to talk to me about screwing girls and the fear inside me was soaring and my heart was breaking.

I knew that day I would be gone from that place, from Ilie and Ancuta, in a short time.

Chapter Twenty-Three

That night I left for the last time.

The mood had been angry all day, with Ancuta glaring and slapping and complaining at and about everyone. She was drinking from early, maybe about 2pm or so, and was soon drunk. She always drank a lot but sometimes it was as if she was not drunk; she never lost caution or dropped her guard. But that day she was slurring her words, calling Ilie a 'bastard' and checking herself in the mirror again and again and again. 'He is the bastard not me,' she said to herself, looking into a hand mirror and sitting at the table.

Skinny had a new bruise on her shoulder and Ilie was coming and going and saying he wanted to grab one of his new Swedish contacts by the throat.

'Too many liars in this world,' he said to Ancuta, but she just snarled back.

For my own sake, for 10,000 reasons, I had to go. On that day I had two things I did not have before: hope and courage. They collided, came together in those hours, and I could not let that feeling pass by. I was strong and I did not know how long it would last.

By around 6pm or 7pm, at that flat in south Belfast, it was quiet. The after-work assholes had been in for their pleasure and there was a lull in time before the next assholes would get in touch.

I went to the bathroom, then to the bedroom. I took the red hoodie and grey jogging bottoms, brought to me by Ilie, from under the bed. I took them back into the bathroom. My heart was beating a little harder as I took my robe off and put the clothes on. It was beating harder, but feeling it made me feel a little bit more alive than I had done in a long time. I put the robe on over the clothes.

Ancuta shouted something, maybe at someone down the telephone, and I knew she would be calling for me at any second.

There were flip-flops, the pair she always flip-flopped around in, at the side of the shower unit. I put them on, stealing one of her most favourite things. I took a very deep breath and walked into the corridor.

I heard her talking to Vali, saying something about someone who needed to learn a lesson.

He spoke back. Ilie was, I hoped, still in there too, drinking his whisky, thinking about someone, distracted by his anger or greed or ambition.

I stood at the door and knew when I opened it the noise would be picked up in a second. Ancuta could be as drunk as a whole bar but, like a cat, she would still hear the noises she needed to hear. It was a heavy, brown door, a strong internal apartment front door, and the sound of it opening and closing was the sound of her business.

She laughed at something, and Ilie laughed. Vali spoke louder, as if trying to talk over their laughing.

And I pressed the handle, pulled the door open a little and slipped out. I did not close it.

I took the steps, in my red dressing gown, and I worried that I might fall over in her flip-flops.

It took me maybe one minute to get to the bottom, to open the door to the outside. A man was coming in and I think when he saw me I must have looked terrified. I was paralysed, just for a second, with the fear that he might be one of the pimps, or some friend of Ilie's, or someone who knew me and knew where I was supposed to be. I was terrified he might just grab my throat or my hair and demand to know where I was going or who had said I could go and do something.

But he just smiled, maybe thought it was funny that I was wearing a dressing gown.

'Hi,' he said.

'Hi,' I said.

And that was it.

The door closed and I was at the front of the building, looking into the November evening darkness and the drizzling rain.

My next fear of course, if they had not already realised I was gone, was that they would see me on the street. The blinds were almost always drawn on the apartment window, but what if they had pulled them open? The window looked directly down to where I was and they would know me immediately. And, of course, if they had already realised I was gone the blinds would definitely be open.

I took off the dressing gown where I stood and then I took off my glasses. I put the glasses in my hoodie pocket and rolled the dressing gown into a ball. I tucked it under my arm like it was a bag. I didn't know what else to do with it. I pulled the hood up, put my head down and walked away from the door, towards the end of the street and onto the Lisburn Road.

My ears were within the hood so I was thinking that maybe I would not hear so well if someone came running behind me. I tucked it back a little, behind my ears, just to try to hear what I might need to know.

If someone had come running and called, 'Hey, blind one,' I don't know what I would have done. I may have frozen to the spot or I may have run like the wind. I did not know if I could run, though, as I had not done such a thing in so long. I had not run, not properly stretched my legs and used all my muscles, in months and months. I don't think I even knew how many months. But here I was now, walking quickly, even running a little, for the first time in all that time. The cold wind and rain was in my face and I was moving forward. I have to tell you it was as scary as it was exciting. It was as normal for anyone in the world as it was completely crazy for me.

So where was I going? I was going into the city centre and I knew the way. I put the dressing gown in a bin and put my glasses on my face. I was sure I knew the streets, the busy parts, where the traffic lights were, and would not take a wrong turn. I walked fast past some of the places I had driven past before – a big bar, a Subway sandwich shop, a Chinese takeaway, a school. It worried me that I was on the main road but it worried me too that, if I stepped off the main road and went through some smaller streets, I would get lost. A lost girl stands out a thousand miles to pimps who know every detail about her. I did not want Ilie trying to work out where I might be because I knew he was so very good at such things.

I kept wiping at my glasses, as the rain wet the lenses. I wanted to be sure I was going the right way, that I was not missing any streets I should not miss. The cars had lights on, some going slow, some going faster, and I could not see inside any window. I could not know if any of them were going to be someone I did not want to see. So I put my head down as much as I could and kept walking, fast, with as much purpose as I ever had in my life.

I got to the city centre, to what is called Great Victoria Street, and I walked towards the City Hall. It was quite busy here but I still felt like I stood out, the Romanian flip-flop girl in red, walking and running and not looking at anyone.

I felt if I was grabbed, once again grabbed from behind, it would be busy enough for it not to be noticed. I wondered if people would come to my aid or if people in this place would just watch and wonder as a girl was pulled into a car and slapped and punched. I could not know and I did not want to find out.

On I went, crossing at traffic lights – beep, beep, beep – and running along towards where the courthouses are. I turned left, just where all the cars turn left, and ran forwards towards the Cathedral Quarter area.

And you know it was here, so close to where I was going, that I remember turning round for the first time to see if anyone was watching me, following me. And there were just people and the lights of traffic and umbrellas and no one at all interested in me. One car that went past was a police car, white and orange, bright colours, and I remember looking quickly away and dropping my head again. I don't know why. Maybe because the police were some part of the world I was trying to leave, maybe because the police had never helped me, maybe because the world would be better for them if I was not a missing girl but a girl who was with the people she was supposed to be with – the pimps and the assholes. I think maybe most of all, though, I turned away from the police because I was, of course, a criminal.

I got to Andy's flat and looked up but could see nothing – no lights, no life. But then maybe I was not looking at the right place. I didn't know for sure. But I was pleased I had made it to where I had wanted to get. The next problem could be dealt with when it happened, but for now I had achieved one, big thing.

I pressed on his buzzer and there was no answer.

The time was, maybe, about 7pm or 8pm. I didn't know. But I did know one thing. He had to be back, in his flat, by midnight because he had a tag on his ankle that gave him no choice. At the most I had four or five hours to wait. I would just have to wait. I would have waited 20 hours or 40 hours or 100 hours, as long as it was just waiting. I was not waiting to be raped, so in a way it was easy to sit, do nothing, say nothing.

I walked around a little bit and thought about things. If they come looking here, I must see them first, I considered. There is a big church, St Anne's Cathedral, and a square opposite it called Writer's Square. If they come looking in the Cathedral Quarter they will be at some point in that place or passing that place.

So I went to the square, to one part of the square where there are little walls near a place where there is a little tiny street onto the next street, and stayed there for a long time, watching all around. I was as dark and hidden as I could be from the road, my eyes darting from one car to another, my head telling me this car was safe, that this one is not Ancuta, this one is not Ilie, not Vali.

In my pocket my fingers played with SIM cards, turning them over and over, moving them around in my hands like little toys. These were the cards I had taken from so many phones, the evidence, the proof of what had been going on, the trail I needed to leave.

I sat on that little wall and tried to look like no one, like nothing, and no one came over to me.

As more time went by there were fewer and fewer people. I saw some who were maybe alcoholics walking through the square and shouting and pushing each other, but none of them bothered me one bit. Strangers were not the people who concerned me that night.

I did not see Ancuta, nor Vali, nor Ilie. I did not even see anyone who looked like them. I had feared my brain would play bad tricks and tell me, 'There she is,' or, 'Run now!' but it did not. I was careful and cautious and I was not alarmed by any car driving slowly or any stranger who looked at my face.

You know what I did think? What a fool I had been. I had been too impulsive, too quick. Why did I not take cash? I was thinking, 'I could have taken maybe a few hundred pounds from the table if I was smart and brave enough, earlier in the day.'

And that would have made it easier, would have made it better for me in terms of food or shelter or even in terms of talking to Andy, but I had not done that. I had left with nothing but SIM cards. I had made them a fortune, been their million-dollar girl, and had earned nothing but damage.

It was maybe two hours later when I first went back to Andy's apartment and buzzed up, but once again there was no answer.

And it was maybe another hour before I was back, standing at his door, buzzing again.

The excitement had left me. The reality of having nothing and nowhere was becoming clear. By now, I knew, Ancuta would be spitting my name and threatening to cut my throat. I knew she would have called my mother and told her what a 'blind bitch' I was. I knew by now that, if Ancuta did find me, she would beat me as hard as she could beat anything with her hard fists.

I stayed closer to the apartments at that stage, my back to a wall, standing in a corner, watching around me all the time, missing nothing. I was by now soaked and hungry as hell and cold and worried. I was getting more worried. I didn't know what would happen next and that was scary in its own way.

And maybe 20 or 30 minutes passed and I heard the happy voices of men and women coming towards where I was standing.

I could see them in the light, carrying bags of drink and laughing, about five or six people all having a good time. I saw Andy there and knew he had come back to meet his curfew.

But, you know, I had no idea in the world what he might say to me, even if he would remember who I was. I had not seen him in weeks and I was just a girl, just a bruised prostitute, who he had met in the course of doing his work.

I walked towards them and they all looked at me, like a wet, sad case of a person.

Andy said, 'Jesus Christ, what are you doing here?'

I said, 'You remember me?'

He said, 'Yes, of course. Natalia. Of course I remember you. Are you okay?'

I saw one of the other men there too. He was nodding, also recognising me.

I know I was crying when I said, 'I need help. Can I ask you for help?'

And Andy said, 'Of course, no problem. Come on upstairs and we'll take it from there.'

'Okay,' I said, and the tears and rain were all over my face.

You know what makes me smile was that there was a party in his apartment. There were already people there, drinking and dancing and singing, when we all arrived. I had been outside for hours and I had no idea. No one had been answering the buzzer or showing themselves at the windows. But behind the black blinds, there was happiness and joy and freedom.

And it was so warm, just like walking into the inside of a big, bright oven. It was so warm and happy and people were laughing.

Lots of people were doing drugs. I have to tell you that there was nothing discreet about it, that people were openly snorting cocaine off tables and off the top of a sound system. Some people were dancing with their eyes wide as if they were on ecstasy. And now the others had come back, including me, and they were taking all the drinks out and putting more into the fridge and starting to take drugs themselves.

'Are you all right?' Andy said to me.

I told him, 'Yes, I had to get away and I don't know where to, I don't know anyone, I can't trust anyone.'

'Well,' he said, 'you can trust us. Don't worry, don't you worry.'

There were crisps and some sorts of party food on the tables.

He said, 'Do you want to get a drink? Get something to eat? It's a bit mental just now but sure we can chat later. Just relax, okay, Natalia? Take your wet jacket off and hang it over a radiator or something.'

And I said I would.

I said, 'My name is Anna.'

'Anna?'

'Yes, from Romania.'

'Okay,' he said, 'nice to meet you, Anna.'

I took some pieces of food for myself, and tried not to look like a starving refugee. I wanted to take off my clothes, but you know I only had bruises and lingerie underneath and I didn't want to show all of that. So I took my little pieces of food and wondered if I could find a room.

A girl spoke with me, Andy's girlfriend, and I remembered we had met before. She told me her name is Fiona. She said I should get out of my wet clothes and I said I would.

She said she hated the sound of my pimps and told me, 'There's dangerous people everywhere.'

And I said I knew this was true. And I knew that just because it was warm and friendly in this place right now it did not mean it could not change to being cold and nasty. You just do not know in this world.

The two bedrooms were busy with people fucking and singing and taking drugs. I went into the bathroom and ate a little bit but my stomach was not liking it. It was empty but full of butterflies and it was so unused to eating much at all that trying to eat it fast made me feel sick.

I could not find peace with people coming and going so I sat down in a hallway and stopped making eye contact with anyone. After a while I got up again and went back into the bathroom and locked the door. There was an en suite in one of the bedrooms and people were also using that. I was just going to steal this room for myself.

I got into the bath and lay down. The noise was a little quieter in there. It was music and laughter and sometimes people turning the handle and trying to get in. But you know I turned the light off and I was able to sleep after a little while, even though I was thinking so much now about dangerous strangers.

You know, this was the first time I had been in a bath in nine months. I love baths and thought it would have been lovely to lie in there when it was full of hot water. But I was too tired to think sensible things and lay in it in my wet, cold clothes.

All of this had been a big gamble, a risk taken on a hunch with people I did not know. But it was away from the worst people in the world, so it was better, miles and miles better, than what I had before.

Maybe it was about 6am when I woke and that was a good long sleep for me. It was quieter but there were still people awake and music was still quietly playing.

I went into the corridor and really wanted to change my clothes. They were smelly and still wet and making me feel so ill.

Andy was not there, nowhere I could see, and I went towards the kitchen area. Someone said 'hello' and I said the same back. I looked in the fridge and there was nothing but beer.

A guy started talking to me about something I do not remember and then asked me, 'Are you hungry?'

I said I was. He said I could order a Chinese, that he could get one delivered at that time.

I said that would be great. He asked what I wanted and I told him what I had to tell him, that I didn't have any money.

He said, 'No problem, love, we're getting a pile of stuff and we can all share it anyway.'

'Okay,' I said, 'thank you. I will have anything.'

I went back to the bathroom and looked in the cupboards, looking for something to wear. There was nothing. And when I was sitting in the kitchen a little later, before the food arrived, Andy's girlfriend, Fiona, came to me again.

'You still here?' she said, as if she was happy to know this.

'Yes, I slept a little in the bathroom.'

'Oh my God,' she said, 'do you need some clothes? You've been in those all night.'

And she got some for me, a yellow T-shirt and a pair of jeans, and like the poor refugee, I went to change.

Afterwards I sat on a stool, smiling, sort of happy and sort of embarrassed, and waited for the food to come.

I had put the lingerie, the only underwear I owned in the world, into the bin.

Chapter Twenty-Four

As the new day started, as I came to realise I was in a new situation, I really felt that I wanted to talk to my mother. I was in among a lot of people from Belfast and found it difficult to understand what was being said. The accent is strong and the words come fast. Sometimes people looked at me and said something about me or to me and I missed what it was. I found that frightening.

Andy had been in and out and seemed to have forgotten me until he saw me sitting on his sofa in his girlfriend's clothes.

'Anna,' he said, 'how're you doing?'

I asked him if we could speak and he said it was not a problem.

The people I had been trafficked by, I said, were still in Belfast and were still doing what they did, but I had left them. I said that I could not live there any longer.

We drank coffee on stools and he asked me more about them, about Ilie, Ancuta and Vali, about the people who came and went, about their connections and contacts. And I told him. It was clear to me, as I had earlier suspected, that he and his people had a problem with them.

'What do you want to do?' he asked.

I did not know what he meant. I thought he had a plan, that he just wanted information from me.

So I told him all I could really want was to make sure I was safe, that I was worried, that I was sorry to bring this all to his door but I felt I had nowhere else to go.

And then I said, 'But, you know, I want to call my mother.'

'Of course you do,' he said.

He handed me a phone, told me to call whoever I needed.

I took the phone to a window and looked out at the street and at rooftops and I rang the home phone number. I did not know her mobile. It was maybe around lunchtime in Romania and I didn't know if she might be working.

The tone of the ringing phone excited me, made me feel as if it was the last sound I heard before something good and beautiful happened. I had many problems with my family, with my mother, with Petre, but all that did not matter at this moment, this was something different. I did not know what I would say because I had too much to say, but just to hear her voice would have been enough.

And it was Petre who answered.

'What has happened?' he said. 'Who have you annoyed?'

I asked him what he meant.

He said the family had taken phone calls in the night, with people saying if I got in touch to tell them I had caused many problems.

'We get all these phone calls about you,' he said, 'and the pictures of you doing all those things.'

I told him he did not know what he was talking about and asked to speak to my mother.

'Your mother is terrified,' he said, 'these people have destroyed our happiness, always ringing up and sending over pictures.

'What have you done? Are you crazy on drugs? Why have you not called your mother?'

I felt so angry, so furious I could have punched a hole in the window. This man was not my father, not even a relative.

'I want to speak with my mother,' I said. 'Get my mother now.'

'She does not want to speak with you,' he said. 'She is only getting some sleep now after the phone calls and the threats all night long.'

He asked me where I was and I said, 'In Ireland.'

And he said, 'Oh yes, they say you have been fucking all the Irishmen for money. So are you a good prostitute? Is that what you are? You left Romania to be a prostitute?'

I told him I would call back to speak to my mother and he told me not to.

'Leave her alone,' he said, 'she is worried for her life and my life because of you. You are dead to us, do you understand? You are dead.'

I don't remember which of us ended the call.

Tears were pouring out of my eyes. It was maybe the hardest slap in my face I had ever had.

Over all the time, you see, the pimps had kept me alive in people's minds, made an image of me, a story of me that did not involve the real me. It was a story where I had been lost, where I had volunteered to cut off all contacts with everyone, including my mother, and to sell myself for sex. It was a story where I was not missing, not taken, not gone, but alive and working and travelling Ireland to be a fantasy for Irishmen. And they had pictures to prove it, my ID to prove it. In this story of theirs, I was not a missing girl, not a trafficked girl, I was just a girl who chose to be a prostitute. I had just found myself on the terrible end of an argument about my life that I did not start. I would have to argue that I was not a prostitute, yet for nine months I had been nothing else. I think I knew from the start that this would have been happening, that there would be a story, that a trail would have been made which told a tale that was not true. And I felt guilt about what I had become, real, stupid guilt for the first time.

Andy told me I could stay for a while if I liked. I could, he said, sleep on the sofa and eat and drink what I liked. He said he knew I understood he was a businessman and that he was always busy, but that he would make sure I was okay for a while if that was what I needed.

He told me he would be telling some people, some of his closest people, that I was with him, as in that I was something like a girlfriend to him, and they would understand. He said he had a few girlfriends and that, because he was with them, then no one asked any questions. If I was just some girl who showed up and hung around, he said, there would be questions and it could get crazy.

'You're with me, okay?' he said.

'Okay,' I said.

Fiona spoke with me later and offered me more clothes.

She told me I was so skinny, as if it was something I should be proud of. I explained I had lost a lot of weight as a trafficked woman. I had been hungry for months.

'Sorry,' she said.

'It's fine,' I said.

But it was awkward.

I was there for two days, confused and quiet, before we all had to move on. Andy had some problem with the landlord and the three or four people who were living there, including me, all had to go.

The night before we left, it seemed like Fiona picked a fight with me. I didn't understand. She said I couldn't just stay for however long I liked and that I should move on.

I told her I wanted to move on. She said she knew I had not been outside since the moment I came into the flat and I said I didn't have the courage to go outside.

'I am in trouble with the people you know about,' I said.

'Well, that's not our problem, is it?'

'I don't know where to go,' I said.

'Go and get on a plane, go home,' she said.

'I am too scared, I have nowhere to go there,' I said. 'I do not even have a passport.'

She was drunk and nasty and maybe, I thought, feared that I was a prostitute who had turned up to try to bed her boyfriend when she was not there. That was not part of my plan. I didn't want sex with anyone ever.

All I wanted to do was find my feet, bring together all my courage, get a sense of what was happening and then I wanted to move on. That conversation with Petre had cut me so deep that I had found myself stopped and stunned, hardly able to think about anything else. If I could have crawled into a little space away from the world, I would have spent a very long time in it.

I phoned my mother's house one or two more times and there was no answer. When we all moved to that new flat, near College Square, I remember calling again and Petre answered again.

I asked to speak to my mother again and he said she couldn't talk. He said not to call back and hung up.

I used Andy's laptop to find my Facebook account and saw it had been shut down after the user, although not me, had posted pornographic pictures. I emailed them and explained and applied for it to be unblocked, and that happened soon after.

Who had done that? Ilie, of course. How had he got my password? I do not know. But I can tell you, when I was taken, I left behind a laptop in my room in London, where Marco was staying. And on that laptop my Facebook password was saved.

Many of my online friends had stopped following me and there were messages saying that I must have gone crazy. My old friend Mirela was one of two people who asked on Facebook if I was okay. The other was my mother.

I sent both of them messages and said I would love to see them soon, that I would explain things later. I said I was sorry if there had been any problems because of me.

My mother got back to say she feared for my sanity, for my health, that she could not even dare to think what I had ended up doing after becoming some kind of drug addict in London. I would have to advise her, she said, of who all the people were who wanted to kill her and Petre and if they were serious. She told me they were changing their number because the calls were coming all the time.

I told her I would ring her now and she answered. It was the first time I had properly heard her voice in nine months.

I could hear her breathing and it brought me to tears.

'I'm sorry,' I said, 'I have to tell you that you will not believe what has happened to me and I want to come home to you.'

She said that would not be a good idea, that Petre had found out more about the people who had been ringing them and that he feared they were genuine killers.

'It is the next thing from the phone calls,' she said, 'that they come and kill you when your daughter has betrayed them.'

At that moment the sadness left me; it just turned to anger.

I said, 'Then you tell those people I am dead. You tell everybody I am dead. Tell Petre I am dead. And to you, I am dead. It's obviously what you all want. You can forget about me and get on with your life.'

I hung up and shouted and cried and wanted to be that dead girl. I had no money and nobody. All I had in the world was the support of a drug dealer in Belfast whose girlfriend was starting to hate me.

What was I to do?

I was told I could sleep on the sofa in the new flat and it would not cost me anything. Andy said he hoped I could get things sorted out in the meantime, and that he understood my life was complicated. He said he would not add to my problems.

'But you can help me out if you like,' he said.

With what?

'You can drive, can't you? You drove yourself and your pimp to my last flat two times,' he said.

I told him that was true, that I could drive.

'I need someone to help out with a bit of driving,' he said, 'and I'd be really happy if it was you.'

'No problem,' I said. What else was I to say?

But nothing happened. A day, maybe two days went by and I was still indoors all the time, waiting for nothing, for something. Fiona came and went and we began to speak a little. She told me she had been drunk and didn't mean to threaten me. She said she had been through a hard time.

Another guy came and went and another girl who asked me, out of the blue, if I wanted to go get a coffee. And you know that seemed like the most normal thing in the world, a good way to help make a friend and just relax in the city, but something inside me was not brave enough. I feared going outside. I hated being inside but was terrified of outside. I didn't know it until that moment – I could not go with her.

Then Andy asked me to drive him somewhere, to an address on the outskirts of Belfast. He told me he knew the way, that he would direct me from the passenger seat.

We went downstairs to his car, his Ford, parked on the pavement outside. We were right in the city centre at this location, although the flats were a little way back from the main streets. But you know I was looking all the time around me on those streets, to where people were walking and gathering, because I was thinking all the time about the face of Ilie, of Vali, of Ancuta.

Andy had a bag, like a little rucksack, in his hand. I didn't see what was in it or wonder what was in it. I had my own thoughts about this.

Do you think it would have been wise for me to ask?

No, of course not. If you want the truth, I didn't give a shit what was in that bag. I had other things to think about. I didn't even ask him if he did not drive, or could not drive, and he did not offer to explain. When all things are considered, I knew at that time it was good for me that I was doing something useful for him.

I drove him to a house and he got out with his rucksack, told me to wait. I sat in the car, a quiet street, and looked in the mirrors, checking here and there, making sure no one was approaching me. It was maybe 20 minutes before he came back alone with his little rucksack.

He got back in and said he wanted to go to another address where he said a friend was living. It was on the other side of the city.

'Would have been too much hassle taking the bus,' he said, and then, 'Thanks, Anna.'

I said, 'It's not a problem. The only problem is driving on the other side of the road.'

'Oh yeah,' he said, 'well you're doing fine.'

He said his friends had been watching Ilie and Ancuta. He said he was still in touch with their business and was very interested in them.

'More than ever,' he said.

'Why?' I said. 'You want to do business with those people?'

'No,' he said, 'we want to stop them doing business.'

'Okay,' I said.

'You can help,' he said.

It was the next day or the day after that I went with one of his friends to a shop. The friend was called Mark. Andy had given me £50 and said to go and get a new top or some shoes and I drove with Mark to Victoria Square shopping centre. I had said I didn't want to go alone and he said Mark would take me.

He asked me, 'Are you and Andy an item?'

I didn't know what to say, after what Andy had said about him telling people we were close.

I said, 'I don't want to talk about that.'

He told me, 'That's fine. I understand.'

A few hours later Andy was taking some cocaine and offered me some, and I said no. He shook his head at me, told me he thought I was a strange person. 'You never do a line?' he said.

'No,' I said. 'I don't think it would be good for me.'

'No good for you to relax, ease some of that tension that's written all over you?'

'But it doesn't ease tension,' I said. 'You must understand, I don't want drugs. Maybe some day, not today.'

'No problem,' he said. Then he thought for a bit, spoke with some guy, turned to me.

'I found out your pimps,' he said, 'are in the Ibis Hotel.'

I shrugged. I didn't know where that was. He pointed to the window.

'Go and look,' he said. And I did. And yes, of course, the Ibis Hotel, Castle Street, was just visible from this flat.

The pimps – the men – would take a hotel room or two and the girls – and Ancuta – would be based in a different hotel somewhere not too far away. In this case, Ancuta and the girls had moved from Windsor Park to the Malone Lodge Hotel, which is not far. Ilie and Vali and whoever he was working with had checked into the Ibis and were coming and going all the time.

Andy said, 'They change location every two or three days, but they're still in Belfast. Is that normal?'

I shrugged. 'Maybe,' I said. 'You can never know what the pattern will be. Ilie was happy that he was setting up business in Northern Ireland and that it was going well. He has made connections in Belfast and Sweden and maybe he is staying here longer than he would before.'

'Or maybe,' said Andy, 'he's hoping to find out where you are so he can get you back before he leaves Belfast.'

Again I shrugged.

'Maybe, but I don't think so,' I said. 'He would not put too much time into it. If I was gone I was gone. I am no threat to him.'

Andy nodded his head at me and smiled.

He said, 'Well I fucking am.'

It was a combination of money and pride and some sort of revenge.

The money was straightforward because Andy and his friends had worked out that the pimps must, at certain times, have thousands in cash with them. They worked out that, often with one of the girls, they go to Western Union and other services to transfer money to Romania or Sweden two or three days a week.

And they worked out that if they got them all together, and timed it so they had not been to Western Union in two days or more, then they would have lots of cash.

The cash would be, of course, all in used notes and the people who had that cash would not, of course, go running to the police if it was taken from them.

There was also pride because I can tell you that Andy really did not like the idea of these women-beating men parking up in Belfast and trying to dominate as much as they could. He had hated it when I said Ilie liked to boast that he was starting to own a part of Belfast and, I think, he could not let it go because it was, to him, a challenge to his pride.

And there was a little bit of revenge because he had seen what Ilie and Ancuta and Vali had done to a trafficked girl and he wanted them to learn a lesson. It was maybe a little bit like he felt protective of me or sorry for me and this was how he demonstrated that sort of thing.

As for the interests of his own friend in running high-class hookers, I don't know. Whatever became of all of that was never told to me.

He asked me if I wanted anything said to Ilie or to the other men.

'What?' I said. I had no idea.

'Anything you want us to say to them, to do to them?'

'No,' I said. 'What are you planning to do?'

'To move them along,' he said. 'If you want anything in particular done to them, to Ilie, you just say so and it'll be done.'

I shook my head. I couldn't think. Were he and his people going to go and attack Ilie and his people? Yes, they were. I couldn't think of anything I wanted for myself when it came down to it. But I did think that I hoped Ilie, Vali and, when she heard, Ancuta and all of their evil friends were going to have a very bad experience.

In the evening time, two or three friends of Andy's came around and they talked, discussed, did some cocaine and left.

They met with some others, some people they were talking with on the phone before they went, on the street. I saw all of them get into two cars, drive to the hotel.

I did not see what happened, of course, but I can tell you what I was told.

All of the men, maybe six men, went to the hotel room in the Ibis and knocked on the door. They made sure they had Ilie and Vali and one other Romanian pimp who had been working with them. They told them to hand over everything they had: cash, weapons and all but one phone, and they took them. Then they told Ilie to make one last phone call to Ancuta to tell her it was over, that Belfast was not a place they could work anymore. Then they took that phone. They walked them down the stairs, outside and to the two parked cars.

They drove them through the city centre and onto the Ormeau Embankment and pulled in at a little park, where you can stop and look at the River Lagan flowing past. They took them out of the car and made them all lie down on the floor, face down. Then they kicked them, punched them and dug their heels into them. They pulled them by the backs of the heads and slammed their faces onto the tarmac. They made those men lie there and take it and they had no choice.

I have been told by someone that one of Andy's gang had a needle, a syringe of heroin, and that he jammed it into the back of Ilie's leg, filling him with the drug before driving away.

And now that would have been a crazy sight, if it was true. Ilie staggering around talking Romanian, passing by people walking their dogs and him with blood streaming from his face. It would have been a very difficult thing for Ilie to get his head together after all of that. But I don't know if that really did happen. I like to think about it sometimes though.

I don't know the sequence of events after that, the moves that Ancuta and Ilie chose to make. But I do know that it was not too long before their base was moved to Sweden and that Ilie can no longer have thought he was such an important man in Belfast.

Chapter Twenty-Five

Andy said I would have full use of the Ford, a huge thing called a Galaxy, while I was working for him. He told me that it was easier if he did not drive and instead that he had a trusted driver. I did not ask why.

There were not what you would call parties in his flat, but in the evenings some people would come round and watch TV and chat and drink and at times do cocaine. I became like part of the furniture there, sitting around day after day with nowhere else to go.

My friend Mirela and I were speaking now on Facebook. I had to ask her if she felt what had happened to me was my fault, if she thought all the things she had heard were true, and she said, 'Of course not.' That was wonderful to hear.

Do you know this? After I was taken, my friend Mirela was the only person to contact my mother to ask where I was.

She contacted everyone, including Marco, to ask if I had been seen. Marco had said I was working funny hours in strange places and that he had no right to know where I was or what I was doing. But Mirela remained suspicious and never believed the story was as simple as that. I love her for that to this day.

'We have to meet,' I told her.

'Yes,' she said, 'I cannot wait to see you again.'

At some stage I would have to get home. I spoke to my mother at Christmas and she said it was not a good time. She said the threats were not as common now but that Petre would not forgive me. I said I would have to arrange something soon. She asked me if I had any money and I had to tell her the truth.

'I have nothing,' I said.

Andy began to pay me for driving. He would reach over now and then in the car, twenty pounds here and thirty pounds there. I would say, 'Thank you,' and he would say nothing else.

He broke up with his girlfriend, had another one and then broke up with her too all in a short time. The girls came and went from his apartment and the men came and sat around and talked about football and people they liked and hated and took drugs.

The days were okay, had little meaning, but it was never the case that I was truly unhappy. I knew that life could be much worse. The daily pressure, the hourly stress I had been under, had loosened. The things I had to do now were so different. I was moving slowly and cautiously and it was as if I was resting.

'Anna,' I would hear at any time of the day, 'can you take me to Lisburn?'

'Anna,' he would say, at 2.30 in the morning, 'I need you to do a wee run with me to Ballymena.'

'Anna,' at 7am, 'we need to get to north Belfast and then to Derry, okay?'

'Anna,' he would say on Sundays, 'I need to go to my mum's.'

And every time I said, 'Okay.'

I would clean my teeth, pull on a jumper and jeans – I had built up a little clothes collection – and we would go.

I knew he was not what you might want to call a really good person. I was sure he was selling a lot of drugs and buying drugs and meeting with people who were not the best people in the world, but I liked him. He never tried to make a move on me in any sexual way and he never asked me things that he knew I did not want to talk about. Some of his friends were crazy, mad as can be, but he had a level head and I think they saw him as the leader because he always had ideas and an easy way of dealing with people.

I had no idea how much of a big or a small fish he was in his world but for me he was not a shark, not an evil person. Was he dangerous? I am certain he was. But bad to his heart? No. He was one of the nicest men I had met in a very long time. I was eating, I was being given money and I felt protected. If you don't have those things, believe me when I tell you that you will like the person who gives them to you.

He told me the police could appear at any time and he knew that worried me.

'Don't worry,' he said, 'just make sure you didn't see anything or hear anything and that, of course, your English is terrible anyway so what could you have heard.'

After a while my fear of the outside was growing and my sleeping pattern started to become increasingly erratic. It had no regularity for a long time and it was not getting any better. But you know I think the main reason it was bad was that I was just so afraid. I was afraid of my own shadow. My once strong heart had become so small, had shrunk down to the size of a stone.

The reminders were all around me. I had brought with me some of what I had left behind. I was moving away from that life before but you know I still sometimes had sore teeth and blood coming out of my mouth. You know, I felt aggressive sometimes for no reason, like something was bothering me when I couldn't say exactly what it was, like a mosquito always flying around my head making me snap or get angry at any moment. I was a person with no hope and nobody and someone who was trying to make that sound okay in my mind because I was not being raped every day of my life over and over again.

I was a person who was sleeping on a sofa in a drug dealer's flat. I was a person wearing tracksuits and driving to towns I had never heard of at all times of the day and night, and someone who was afraid to walk to the shop.

One girlfriend of Andy's asked me about my teeth, asked me why I had blood on my lips. I told her my head had been closed in a door, that I had been slapped in the mouth a lot. I said I had learned to not eat with the back of my mouth, learned that the pain came and went and to live with it.

'Oh my God,' she said, 'are you crazy – you need a dentist.'

But I didn't know anything about getting a dentist and I didn't know if I needed money or a passport or what to do. I didn't know if I called a dentist whether the police would arrive at the door and arrest me and Andy and everyone else. I had these concerns that might not sound sensible but they were real to me, to a person who cannot go outside.

She got me some antibiotics to deal with the problems in my mouth. It is disgusting but there had been pus and yellow liquid coming from my teeth for a while. I would brush them, brush around the pain, but in my mind I always knew I was building up problems.

But my body had been wrecked so I did think how bad teeth at the back of my mouth did not break my heart. I was looking kind of okay I think, but my mind was shattered and my physicality had changed.

You know that my lower back was still so sore, and is to this day. I was kicked there, punched there, shoved there over and over again. I was pressed there, twisted there, carried weight there over and over and over. I was slapped there and whipped there. If you ask me to stand up, the first thing I will want to know is for how long until I can sit again. If you ask me to go for a walk, I will need to know how far.

My head hurts, at the back, at the skull, from where my hair was pulled 10,000 times. I wear ponytails so often now to hide the lack of growth. My knees are the knees of an old woman. They creak and groan because they have been put under so much pressure so often. Do you want me to tell you why? You work it out.

And inside, in my vagina, in my ass, it does not all work as it should. It is not as if I have the good, healthy system I once had because there is deep damage, deep pains, which I may have to spend the rest of my days trying to forget.

My breasts were pulled and hit and punched so often that I think I lack feeling where once there was a sweet sensitivity. And my stomach has never reverted to its normal self, contracting more than it ever did and sometimes making me feel sick when there is no reason why I should be.

And you know I can always smell it, the bleach and the sweat and the cum, the breath, the armpits, the pants, the assholes.

To this day I still have problems with the streets, with being in public, with being alone on a road even if there are a million other people around. And to this day, my sleep remains a mess, unsettled and unsatisfying.

I had maybe been staying with Andy for six weeks when I met Tom. He was in the bar of the Ramada Encore Hotel and I was there with Andy and some of his friends. It was around Christmas time and there was a nice atmosphere in the place. I had gone to the bar to order some drinks and I was in a pretty good mood because everyone seemed to be in a pretty good mood.

He asked me, this man in a smart suit and with a kind face, if I was having a nice time. I said I was and I asked him the same. He said he was and that he always liked meeting people, chatting to people, especially people who did not come from the area.

'What brings you to Belfast?' he said, and he had this nice smile and a nice way of putting his polite words that made me feel like he really wanted to know the answer. No man really wants to know that answer, you know, at least not the ones who are paying to be with you.

I said, 'You don't want to know what brought me here, trust me.'

He laughed and said he did trust me, and said it was too early for me to think I knew him well enough to know what he might want to know.

'You don't want to say?' he said.

'No,' I said, 'maybe some other time.'

'I'd like that,' he said. He gave me his card and said he worked in the media, that he always liked to hear interesting stories from interesting people.

'Thank you,' I said, 'that's very kind of you.'

I liked him, but I walked away.

Two weeks later and I was driving back from Derry with Andy in the car. It was cold, wet and we were talking about good things to eat on horrible days. I said toast was one of my favourites, and said how I loved butter more than anything, that real Irish butter must be the best in the world. He said that was true, that he loved it, that he loved the smell of hot toast and butter.

I realised we were so low on petrol that we would have to find a filling station. He said there was one a few miles ahead, at the bottom of the big hill called the Glenshane Pass, and I said I remembered it.

Just after, before we reached the start of the big hill, a police car tucked in behind us and flashed its lights. I pulled over.

'Balls,' he said, as two policemen got out and walked to our car. I was asked my name and if I knew the name of my passenger, where I had been and where I was going to. I answered as best I could, in English that was suddenly so broken that no one could understand it.

But the policeman didn't care about me. He was just going through the motions. The main goal of the police was to arrest Andy, which they did about 20 seconds later. He opened his door and they put handcuffs on him at the side of the road.

'Breach of bail conditions,' they said to him, and he cursed.

They searched the car, searched him and searched me before putting him in their car and driving off. He nodded at me, I think he may have shrugged at me, as he was taken back to jail. I learned later he was facing trial for drugs offences. He would not get out again for a long time.

And once again for me a difficult situation had presented itself. I was alone on a main road with no money and a car that had almost no petrol. But I did have a phone.

I called one of Andy's friends and said he had been taken away by the police. He and another man drove from Belfast to pick me up.

'What about the car?' I said.

'Forget it,' they said. 'Sure the cops know it and it's a heap of shite anyway.'

We just left it there at the side of the road.

Back in Belfast, I felt unsure, unhappy about what had happened. I wanted to talk to Andy, to check if I should go or stay or if there was anything I should do to help him.

One friend asked if I was staying or if I was going, as Andy would not be around now.

I said I didn't know.

I cried about this, about his having to go to jail, about my life being turned upside down again. None of his friends seemed to care at all. The next day there was a group of them in his flat, people coming and going, and they were saying they would be moving his stuff out. They told me that because I was Andy's girl I would have to reconsider things. I felt lost.

Later that day I hit a really bad point when the straw blew into my day that broke the camel's back. I dropped my mobile telephone down the toilet and it made me feel so sad and depressed I didn't know what to do. As I tried to fix it later, sitting in the kitchen drying it, with people coming and going and ignoring me, I thought I would see if I could get some help.

Tom had told me he was in the media, that he would hear my story if I told him. It hit me in a flash that this was maybe, just maybe, one man who could understand and maybe even help to explain my situation to others. All I wanted to do was to be able to explain. I was bursting with guilt, with shame, even though I knew I had no real reason to feel that way.

Chapter Twenty-Six

It is a strange thing to call someone you don't know with the hope that they might want to know everything about you. For me at that time, it was as if I was in a perfect storm. I had been trapped, sold, raped and damaged. I had become a criminal. I had no ID. I had so far been unable to explain everything – the losing of myself, the online pictures of me in underwear – to my depressed mother in Romania. I did not feel I could go to the police. I did not feel I could go anywhere. And now, the only person I had come to trust, a drug dealer, was gone.

Was I seeking to unload all of this onto a complete stranger? I think I was. I think I had to. The only way any of my situation made sense was if all of it was explained. I needed someone to know more in the very faint hope they could give me some advice.

I rang Tom and asked if he remembered me.

'Yes, of course,' he said.

'You said that if I wanted to talk to give you a call,' I said.

'Yes,' he said. 'You want to?'

'Yes,' I said. 'Can we meet?'

'Of course,' he said. 'Name the place.'

I was nervous, not just about meeting with him but because I was meeting him on my own. The day before I had left Andy's place and checked into a hotel, a Premier Inn, and started to spend the £200 I had earned from driving and had put to the side.

I think I was shaking a little as we met for coffee in Belfast city centre. We talked about it being a cold day. He asked me about Romania and what I thought of Belfast. I didn't have much to say and I wondered how much I could say to this man who could be anyone in the world.

'You're uncomfortable,' he said. 'I'd go so far as to say you seem like you're scared.'

'I am scared,' I said.

'What of?'

'Everything,' I said. 'I am afraid of the next minute, the next person, the next event in my life whatever that event might be.'

'Is there anything I can do to help?' he said, and I looked at him. I remember the next thing I said to him was bad English, that it did not come out perfectly, but that he understood it.

I said, 'I don't have a nice situation.'

'What's wrong?'

And I began to explain. I began to tell him that I needed someone to help me because I had lost everything, including my pride, my dignity. I said that I had been taken away by some people and I had been sold. I said I had been to court, that I had escaped, that I had ended up driving for a drug dealer and that there was no part of my life that remained clean, remained intact.

I said, 'You know there is not even a Romanian embassy in Northern Ireland. I would like to talk to them about my passport but now you see I am a criminal. And I don't even know if I am in danger in Romania. I don't even know if I want to see my mother again. I don't know anything now.'

Tom said, 'If you could have things just the way you wanted, what would you have?'

'I would have my documents, I would not be a criminal, I would not be in danger, I would have a life, I would study, I would be loved, I would be healthy and I would not have my head full of the darkest things,' I told him.

We sat for a long time. He asked for more detail, to go back to the start, to explain where I had been. I told him I had been a sex slave, a trafficked prostitute, and that I was screwed by thousands of men and I never wanted to be with a single one of them.

He sat back and said, 'This is not real.'

I said, 'What?'

He said, 'I can't believe this. Here – in Belfast? This was happening here?'

And I said, 'Yes. It is happening now, as we sit here, to trafficked women in this city. Do you not understand that?'

He shook his head.

'I never thought … here, right here?'

'Yes,' I said.

'You must go to the police,' he said.

'No.'

'Why?'

'Because the police do not care,' I said. 'You think they care when it is going on in every town? They want only to arrest sometimes a big pimp, they don't care about the girls. What would I say to police? I would say, "Oh hi, I was an escort in Belfast and was beaten by pimps and I also have a criminal record and no money or passport and I was taken from London and I'm a friend of a drug dealer you put in jail so can you help me?" What would they do?'

He said, 'They might go after the pimps.'

And I said, 'And the pimps will then go after me. You don't understand. I am trapped. They build traps that people cannot get out of. I am in danger. There is nothing I can do.'

He said, 'If you want to confront all of this, if you want to explain how all of this happened to anyone, you have to tell the police. People might not believe you otherwise. I would find it easier to believe if you went to the police.'

And that was such a strong thing for him to say. It would be one of the most important things anyone ever said to me.

We met again the next day and talked more. He told me he wanted to help, that he had made some calls and was looking into the situation. He said he wanted to pay for the next night in the hotel and I refused. But he said he only wanted to do that temporarily because, he told me, he would be able to find a flat where I could stay, alone and safe. He promised me. And I have to tell you the relief was beautiful.

'But you must go to the police,' he said.

'I told you I do not want to do that.'

'You must,' he said. 'Think again about this. I cannot believe all of this until you go and tell them, make it formal, get an investigation started. You have nothing to lose. You are the victim of horrendous crime and others are victims of the same criminals. You must go to the police. I believe you have a duty to do so.'

I told him, 'I am a criminal.'

'No,' he said, 'your mind has been twisted. You are trafficked.'

I said, 'I don't trust police.'

'Maybe,' he said, 'you don't trust police in your home country, maybe you had a bad day in Galway with the police, but if you voluntarily come forward with information about these people, about what has happened to you, then you will be fine. I'll go with you. Sound okay?'

It didn't, but it was becoming more and more clear to me that he had a point. His words about not believing me were so significant. I knew I had to go forward, to do something to move things along for myself, for my future, for my sanity.

Tom had a friend who could let me have a flat for nothing for a short time, and that was wonderful news. I think by the time I moved in, which took all of two minutes, I was already feeling stronger. A meeting had been arranged informally with the PSNI's Human Trafficking people. By the time it happened, I had grown more confident. I had walked alone in the city centre for the first time. These were small steps, which were big steps for me. I think that hope is something that gives more hope. But you know, in truth, I did not know for sure what I was hoping for.

We met the police in California Coffee near Belfast City Hall, Tom beside me at the table. Two detectives in plain clothes joined us. One of them was the head of the unit at the time and, Tom told me, he would know what I was talking about more than anyone. His name was Philip Marshall.

Tom went quickly over what I had told him. Mr Marshall listened to all of this and then looked at me. He asked me for my name, about where I was from and some other things. I was not sure he was very interested. He asked me if I knew the names of my pimps and I said I did. He took out a pen and pushed it across the table to me. He pushed a little napkin too, just one that was sitting on the table beside our coffees.

'Can you please write the names of the people you are talking about?' he said.

I took the pen and wrote the names Ilie Ionut and Ancuta Schwarz. I pushed the napkin back to him. He looked at it, then up to me. Then he looked at it again, and back to me. He was stunned. Somehow these names had seized him inside. It was clear he knew them. I knew the police knew of Ilie because they had raided a property – Margarita Plaza – in Belfast with his picture in their hand.

'Okay,' he said, 'right.'

Tom and I waited for him to say something that made sense.

'Right,' he said, turning to his colleague. 'We need to get on to this.'

He looked at me and nodded. 'Okay,' he said, 'we know them. We definitely know them. What I need now is to update all the information we have, update the whole system. Do you follow me? We need to get you in and talk to you. We have a lot we need to talk about. You need to tell me everything.'

There was another meeting after that, and maybe another two after that before we met formally for interviews. The other meetings took place at Ten Square Hotel in Belfast city centre. Other police involved in investigating trafficking and organised crime were there each time. They went through my story in more detail, said they would investigate every single part of it. They said I would qualify for a certificate from the Serious Organised Crime Agency verifying that I was a victim of trafficking. I was placed into the national database and told that, when the certificate was cleared, I would be brought in to give my witness statement.

'Okay,' I said, 'and then what happens?'

I was told that, if all was well, the pimps who destroyed my life, destroyed so many lives, would be tracked down, arrested, prosecuted and jailed.

I said, 'I don't even think they are in this country.'

And a man said, 'It doesn't matter. They are part of an international crime network. We just need someone somewhere to speak out.'

It took three months for the certificate to be issued. The value of it was that I was being taken seriously, that I was not a criminal in the eyes of the PSNI. That meant a lot, a huge amount, to me.

In June, as the interviews began, they told me this was now part of what was Operation Burgrave. It was, they said, a long, ongoing plan to bring down a pan-European sex trafficking operation that had for a time been based in Northern Ireland. Burgrave is an old German word for a military ruler. I have no idea why it was used for this business.

The interviews were another new journey for me. I came in the first time and talked about myself, where I was from, why I moved to London, who I met there and what happened on the day I was taken and flown to Galway. It was detailed stuff, face by face, name by name. It took hours and exhausted me but it was good because they were serious. They spent most of the day with me. And they asked me to come back in three days' time, and two days after that, and the next week, the next week and the next.

By then, I had moved in with Tom. We were sharing a flat, his flat, and our relationship had become close. Much of our time we were researching sex trafficking cases, the law and facts and media reports around the issue. We were looking into how the issue is being dealt with around the world and finding again and again that so little is being done for a problem that is so big and getting bigger all the time.

Tom was looking after me, caring for me, but I wanted to work. I wanted to get out there into the world again and make some money, be a legal, honest, existing person with a name and with friends and a life and a future. But I could find no easy answers as to what rights I had as a Romanian.

One day I went to a doctor's surgery in east Belfast and asked if they could make me one of their patients. They asked what ID I had and I showed them the SOCA certificate. I said I was working with the police. They looked at me as if I was crazy.

'It is the only ID I have,' I told them.

'What is it?' the lady asked.

'It proves I am a legal person here.'

'We can't use that,' she said, 'that's not an ID. That's some police thing. Don't you have any other ID?'

I was so embarrassed. I felt like a cheat, like a fool. I walked out of there with my head down.

One important issue for me was to be checked out for diseases, checked out for HIV, because I had no idea what I might have caught. In time I was able to establish that at an anonymous clinic in Belfast where they check for sexual illnesses. I do not have HIV.

Tom was working so much with his business but we began to do a lot of work together on my situation. It turned out what I needed to do was make sure everything was clear with the tax people so that I could register once again and start paying tax.

I had been on the books in 2010 in London, paying my tax from the cleaning work, but then I had disappeared. I told the tax people what had happened. They told me I could not do anything until I had settled my account. Then they sent me a bill for £2,500. They told me I had not closed off my accounts from 2011 and now it was 2012 and this was the figure outstanding. I could not work or even claim anything.

Another problem.

I went to Dublin, to the Romanian embassy there, and said I hoped to get my papers. I said my passport had been stolen and that I was planning to pay my tax and work legitimately in Northern Ireland.

They told me if I paid them 120 euros they could get me a travel document allowing me to go to Romania, and when I was there I could arrange for a new passport.

'You are not living in the Republic of Ireland,' they said to me, 'so there is not much we can do.'

It was just stupid red tape after red tape.

Something about this situation, even though there was now so much promise, felt at the same time so hopeless. I don't know if that feeling came from my brain or began in my body, but I felt again that I was growing weak. My back – always sore – was getting worse and the once improving sleep was now suddenly getting worse again too. I wanted a doctor for sleeping tablets, I wanted a dentist to look at my bleeding teeth, and getting signed up to these things was taking too long.

By August, I had met with Tom's family. They were good people, good to me and so understanding of all that I was going through. It was his mother who said I must go to my home country to visit. She said there would always be a risk one way or another but that I was unsettled and unwell and under pressure in terms of the meetings I was having with the police.

'Go home and see your mother,' she said, 'it's been too long.'

And I knew she was right.

The police wanted all the details of my travel to Romania. They spoke with the airport people in Bucharest and in Belfast and Tom's mother kindly paid for the flight, a five-day trip.

Police officers came with me to Belfast International Airport and waited until I left the departure lounge. As the plane took off my heart was in my mouth. The last time I had been in my own country, I had been taken there by Ancuta and Ilie and I had been taken to be sold. And I did not get to see my mother. This time, my mother was waiting for me.

My heart was exploding when I saw her at the airport, standing with tears in her eyes. She had a little gift for me in her hands, a little monkey toy for a little girl, and I could not stop crying as I walked towards her. We hugged and laughed and hugged and nothing was said.

The man she was with was a doctor from the hospital where she worked. He said he had heard about me and hoped I was well. I said I was not. He said he had heard I had problems, and my mother had asked him to be there. That was a kind thing to do, a lovely thing to have arranged. It was like she knew what was most on my mind.

I asked her, 'What are people saying?'

And she told me, 'Maybe you don't want to know, Anna. There are people in Romania who make it their business to speak out about people over and over again.'

How come my name was being damned over and over by people I did not know? Could they be people involved in the same business, rapists and traffickers and drug dealers from Sibiu with friends in Bucharest and friends in London and Ireland and everywhere else? Yes of course. I have no doubt in my mind. For criminals, all trafficked women who escape or speak out are disloyal liars, sluts, drug addicts, freaks.

The doctor checked me over and told me I would need to begin proper courses of painkillers. I was not moving my body right, he said, and only making things worse for myself. He said it was clear I had some damage, the worst of it on my lower back, possibly also around my pelvis. I must stretch and do yoga and make sure I moved all the muscles and made them all grow strong again.

I saw a dentist in Sibiu, another appointment that was arranged by my mother. I had told her in a phone call that I had broken teeth. Do you know what he did? He removed four of my teeth in one go.

'They have to come out because they will poison you,' he said, really baffled as to how I broke so many teeth and that I had left it so long. He told me he should not take so many teeth out in one sitting but that he had little choice in my situation. I thanked him so much after, even though my mouth was like a bomb had exploded in there.

'You need to have more removed,' he told me.

I could not even think about that.

There was no heart-to-heart with my mother. We went to her house and Petre was there, looking me up and down like I was an intruder, and he made it clear he was not happy to see me. My mother carried on with things, talking about some people we knew and what had been going on and not looking too much into my eyes at all. I cried on the first day I was there, cried a lot of the night and could not sleep.

Petre went out during the day and my mother went to work. She said she was so busy with work at the hospital that she had no choice. I did not go out, feeling afraid to see people I knew from my past, to see people who thought I had become a prostitute by choice and was giving myself to people all over the world. I would have been ashamed but also furious to meet people who thought that.

In the end, I came home after the five days more unhappy than I had been when I left. It was a disappointing visit. It ended with Petre telling me I had told him once I would not bother them again. I told my mother we needed time and space and that I was working with the police to help catch some big pimps, the people who had destroyed my life, but she did not want to know.

'All of that is terrible stuff,' she said. 'I am so sad that is how things went for you.'

Each time we spoke, when I wanted to speak with her about what had been going on, her eyes would well up with tears and she would turn away and say she had so much to do and so much had changed and so much this and that and things are all different now.

I did not say goodbye to Petre, but I hugged my mother. 'I have so much to say,' I said again, and she said she loved me and hoped things would work out with the police.

I know now that so many evil people, so many nasty, disgraceful people were saying so many things that my mother's life was being made hell, and that Petre really did hope I would disappear forever.

She brought me to the airport and I told her the next time I would hopefully speak more and would not have four teeth out in a single day again.

'I was kidnapped, stolen by those people and I was raped for months,' I said. 'You know that, you know I did not contact you because I could not, you know that? Now I am rebuilding my life, why will you not be my mother again and I will be your daughter?'

She told me Petre was part of her problem, that there were issues in the marriage.

'You are controlled by him,' I said, 'don't you see how bad he is for you? Can you not understand?'

She said, 'I know you're telling me the truth, Anna, about you, about Petre. I just cannot deal with it.'

Chapter Twenty-Seven

I would work with the police for two years, from 2012 to 2014. We met every week at Garnerville PSNI station in east Belfast and I told my story. I spoke for hundreds of hours, testimony on all the crimes I knew of carried out by Ancuta and Ilie.

The PSNI began working with the Metropolitan Police in London and with Europol and EuroJust and the Romanian police. Piece by piece, they were moving forward, and every piece of it was a piece out of me.

There are things I have seen and been through that I cannot talk about, but that I had to talk about. I found myself crying and scared and, of course, I was all alone most of those times. It was a difficult process but I knew always it was the right thing, but I cannot say that knowing that made any of it easy.

I don't like to cry, I am not a girl who cries easily, but the things they needed to know came out of me often with huge difficulty and with tears to go with them.

At times, when I was lucky, Tom was with me and sometimes his mother was there. She talked to the police one time after the sociologist who was working with them, who was putting together some details on the case, was left feeling so deeply disturbed by what I was saying. The sociologist had said to me she felt like she wanted to kill the people who did what they had done to me.

Tom's mother asked the police if they could help make things easier for me with social services and the police said they could not. She said that my story was so upsetting that even the sociologist was left outraged, so why could they not take more care of my feelings?

They said they had to move on, to get everything, no matter how difficult, that their job was to get the evidence they needed.

She said, 'No one is taking care of this girl. You are taking everything and she is left here crying.'

They said they were sorry but they had no choice, and recommended some charities I could speak with.

But, she asked, could they not get someone to sit with me for half an hour after each session? Someone professional just to tell me the things I needed to hear?

They could not. They told me they appreciated this was very difficult but that people in cases of human trafficking are able to help in so many areas of crime. It is all linked, they said, drugs and trafficking and money laundering and organised crime.

The police connected me with a charity helping female victims but it did not work out for me. They told me I had a very high level of trauma and abuse and I said I knew that. I'm afraid it was not a good meeting. I think I traumatised the lady I spoke with. She told me one of my many problems was going to be that I was not rescued, that I had not been 'saved' by the police, that I had escaped from my trafficked life.

'There is a statutory process for rescued victims,' she said. 'However, I appreciate very much that you have been in a horrific situation.'

She advised I speak to someone at a charity that dealt with sexual abuse specifically in terms of managing some of my problems, and I went along to see them too. They seemed confused about my case and I told them they didn't seem to understand what sex trafficking was. They said they had never dealt with such a thing before.

I left that charity too feeling as if I had traumatised them.

Later on the police brought up the prospect, at some possible stage in the future, of my joining a Witness Protection Programme. They said, if arrests were made, I could then appear comfortably in court and testify against my pimps. I had no problem giving evidence against my pimps because I hated these people more than I hated anyone else on earth. So what would I have to do?

I would have to give up forever the people I knew and be taken to a secret address, within the UK, where I would not be able to talk with them ever again.

'My mother?' I asked.

'You could have no more contact,' they said. They said they had no doubt my life would be at risk.

'And so would my mother's,' I said, 'and it is already at risk.'

They knew this was true. But she could not be part of this.

I felt I was being offered nothing for everything. I cannot tell you that I felt this was the right thing to do.

You know, I believe that there were some there who also felt it was not the right thing to do. I have been able to learn since that some police felt I was too angry, a little too damaged to take the witness stand in any future court case, but that was never made clear. However, I think, at that time, they might have been right. People have told me many times that defence barristers 'tear people to shreds' and I don't know how I would have been on any witness stand, being torn to shreds and accused because of things I had no control over. The issue was left open and the interviews continued.

They wanted to know where the money laundering was done from. I told them of the places they used, where they took the cash and where they sent it, how and who and when.

They were interested that Ilie had business connections in Sweden because they believed he was there at the time. The information I was giving, I would find out, was being passed to the Swedish police.

They had some kind of a picture before I came, some insight into Ancuta and Ilie and their business, about where they had been, how they recruited and tricked and twisted and took girls from one life and sank them into another. But if you think of that picture they had, think of it in black and white. When I came along, I was able to give them the colour.

I told them to search escort pictures online in Sweden, in Stockholm, and they would sooner or later find poor Skinny, find Ancuta. It was, I said, the simplest way to find out where they were. This worked.

I asked them about the time the police came to Margarita Plaza, how I was there during that raid when they had pictures of Ilie Ionut in their hands and Ancuta had a mobile phone inside her, but they had no record of that on the files.

They asked me if I was sure that raid took place. What a strange thing to say. I will never understand what happened with that.

I asked about the men, all the thousands of men who ring the phones to book and abuse trafficked women, all the men all over Ireland who keep the business alive, who pay pimps and thieves and kidnappers and rapists to allow them to do what they want to the girls they have got.

There would not be a lot, the police said, they could do about those men. They were interested in the top criminals, they said.

I told Tom about this, about the SIM cards with the numbers of maybe 1,000 callers or more, about not knowing what to do with them. He said he had been thinking about that and how he suspected that handing them over to the police might mean I may never see them again. I did not tell the police that I had these in my possession.

Tom and I decided together to give them to our solicitor, to ask him to store them securely with the hope that one day they will mean more than the nothing they seemed to mean to the police. These were my trail, evidence of where I had been, of what had been, and I was not going to give it away too quickly.

In time the pressure of all the questioning was killing me. No session was less than two hours and in all that time I could be explaining just five minutes of my life. I felt after a while that nothing was going to be done, but I had to finish what I had started.

For a time they focused on what I had been doing after I got away from Ilie and Ancuta, about the man I had spent a lot of time with, about what I had been doing when I stayed at Andy's flat. This was not what I had come to tell the PSNI all about, but all the same they asked. And asked. And asked.

Did I know about his criminal movements, about his drug deals, about the connections he had in Europe? Did I know he was a bad man, a liar, a thief, a man who had a good start in life but who took his wrong turns by his own choice?

I told them I did not. 'I don't know anything about Andy,' I would say. It did seem to me as if they felt they had someone who could help them with information about a man who was already in jail, help build not just one but two pictures of the inside workings of crime gangs.

I have to tell you I could not, would not, did not. You may think what you like to think, but Andy was my friend, a man who was loyal to his word and there for me when I needed it most, a man who may have saved my life.

What do I know about his life, his criminal doings?

Nothing.

A friend of Tom's was able to get me a little job washing dishes in a café in the very centre of Belfast, and I was happy to take it to give my brain and body something new to do. I could pay no tax and I still had a tax bill hanging over me, but I needed to do something other than pour my life out of my heart all the time.

One day, in August 2012, I was waiting outside, close to that café, sitting in Tom's car as he spoke to the man who owned the place, and something came on the radio that got me listening. An anti-human trafficking bill had been put forward at Stormont, it said. One of the politicians up there, an MLA, was putting forward a private members' bill to change the law, to make life harder for sex traffickers, for people who trade people. I laid my head back and closed my eyes and thought for a moment. Then I opened my eyes and said to myself, 'This is what I need to do.'

It was like a little spark of hope, a little piece of clarity, of official sense. I had learned that the whole system seemed not to know what to do with trafficked people. The whole world seemed not to know what it was to be a victim who was kept out of sight, to be someone who was attacked every day in secret over and over. Clarity was needed to state what this was, to make it clear that victims are not criminals, to say that those who do this, those who use these women, are the criminals, are like modern-day slave owners.

Would this law not make life more difficult for the pimps? Would it not strike at their easy, unchallenged way of making money? I didn't know, but I wanted to find out all about it.

I told Tom, 'This law, this proposal, this idea that is being put forward at the Northern Ireland parliament in Stormont, can we help? No one else is doing anything. Can we do something?'

This suggestion lit up his face. He said, 'Yes, of course. This is exactly what we must do.' Tom made an approach to the office of Lord Maurice Morrow, the man who proposed the Human Trafficking and Exploitation Bill. He told him he knew of a victim who had a story to tell, who hoped she could help with the passage of what was going to be a controversial bill into law.

We met with him at his office in Stormont and he asked me for an outline of my situation. He said he supported law change because he was hearing more and more stories of men and women, also of children, being forced to work, of them ending up in Northern Ireland brothels and farmyards and factories.

But, he said, there was a problem in getting this message across. The issue, he said, was not being taken seriously enough because it was not visible.

I could tell his heart was in the right place but that he did not have everything he needed to make his case.

I said, 'If my story can be used to help make things better, then I will do whatever I can. I will speak to anyone you like about my story.'

He said it would be good, firstly, to meet with Peter Robinson. We shook hands and left his office. Outside, Tom said to me, 'Do you know who Peter Robinson is?'

And I knew he was a senior politician in Northern Ireland.

'Yes,' said Tom, 'he's the First Minister. That's as high as you can go.'

What this meant was that, in so fast a time, my story was moving upwards, to the top, to the ears of those who had the power to change things.

'I don't believe this is happening,' I said to Tom.

'It's happening all right,' he said, 'there's a long way to go but we've started well.'

That night we drank champagne and I told him about the faces of Ilie, of Ancuta, of the ugliness of some people, how it comes through from the bones.

An invitation came and a few days later we were at a charity fundraising party in County Armagh where I was introduced to Mr Robinson.

He said, 'We have high hopes for this bill, of bringing in changes that will make a real difference. We want to do what human traffickers don't want us to do, which is make life much more difficult for them. Eventually, we hope others will follow where we lead. I hope you can help with that.'

I told him I believed there was a lot of money in this business, that sex traffickers were making fortunes from selling women's bodies to men. And I said, knowing the business as I did, there would be a fight.

He said, 'But there's always a fight when you are doing something new.'

In a few weeks a meeting was called by the Justice Committee for MLAs who wanted to hear the story of a sex trafficking victim. I was asked to go along, to tell my story and to present my case, tell of my belief why this law was a very good and strong idea for Northern Ireland.

It would be based on the so-called Nordic model and would be a stronger law than in the Republic of Ireland, stronger than anywhere in the rest of the UK, one of the strongest laws in the world against human trafficking. I was very excited to play the strongest part I could in making it happen.

I had a black dress, smart and dignified, and my hair was blonde. I wore a ponytail, because of what had happened to my hair, and I wore new shoes that Tom had bought me for the occasion.

On that day, in that room, there were 12 MLAs, some of whom were not sure if they should support Lord Morrow's bill and some who were already supporting it and wanted to see a true victim, a true survivor, in front of their eyes.

It was exciting and unnerving. Tom told me to speak clearly and confidently and that I was the face and voice of what could be a radical new law for Northern Ireland and I had to think of those suffering, those being raped and beaten right at that moment, as I spoke.

But you know, the police did not like this law. The PSNI did not support it from the start, saying it would result in few prosecutions as it was so hard to enforce. For me the important thing about this law was that it would criminalise men who pay for sex.

Perhaps you think that is wrong and unfair? Maybe you are right. Maybe there are 'happy hookers' out there who make extra money from passing gentlemen and it helps them feed their families. But tell me about the trafficked women? The women brought into Ireland, the UK, brought all around Europe and hidden away in brothels. Tell me about bruised people who appear only on internet pictures and in dark bedrooms when someone has money to pay for them.

Tell me about the women who are beaten, daily, in your town so they make more and more and more money for their pimps. Do they not exist? Are they not being controlled? Are they not being mentally twisted and violated again and again and again? Your sister? No. Your mother or daughter? No. So do you care?

These are someone's relatives and they are being used for profit, sometimes 100 per cent profit, by pimps and they are in the process of losing everything and gaining nothing. If a law comes along that can say the woman is a victim and not a prostitute, then I want that law. Pimps are only interested in the market. The only way to hit the market is to target the buyer. And that is the only way to reduce and, I pray, one day end sex trafficking.

If all of that is bad news for a man who feels he can no longer stop off with a hooker on his way home from work before seeing his wife, then that is just tough luck. The prize is bigger than his need.

You know what is funny? The sex lobby who hate this law. The alliances of sex workers, these 'happy hookers' who seem to forget all about sex trafficking and say they don't like this law because it makes their clients feel bad, feel at risk. They say a law like this only forces people underground, forces them underground and puts them more at risk.

Underground? Are you serious? How underground was I? How much more deep underground can you get? I had vanished, been removed from society.

And this is my case. And this was what I was going to say. And I was going to answer any question anyone would ask.

A detective from the PSNI's Human Trafficking Unit came to Stormont that day and he was not happy. He was distressed that I was going to give my presentation to politicians and there was no input from the police. He felt that was important, that the PSNI did not feel my argument on this matter should be heard in isolation and did not take into consideration all the factors.

I believe what he meant was that catching low-level pimps and prostitutes was traditionally a very good way for the police to get information, because the trade is always connected to bigger criminal networks. But the police concerns about that matter were not my concern.

Whatever the reasoning, he became more and more flustered as he spoke with me and some other people outside the room before we went in.

'We can't have,' he said, 'a prostitute going in and explaining laws in there.'

And I heard every word.

Tom asked for this man to be clear about what he had just said. He left it at that and went away. It was not too long, you know, before he was replaced in his job.

But I had been called a million names that were not mine, and the name of a prostitute was not mine either. Big deal.

I walked into the room with my head held high and I made my case. The session was meant to last one hour. I was there for more than three.

Chapter Twenty-Eight

In April 2013, I was sitting in a room with PSNI officers, talking more about my story. More and more details, more and more locations. And, on that day, a detective came into the room.

'Anna,' he said, 'we have some news.'

'News?'

'Yes,' he said. 'We have just arrested Ancuta Schwarz.'

And my heart danced inside me. 'Oh my God,' I said. 'Where?'

'Belfast.'

She was back. They had been to Sweden where they had been building their horrible empire. As I already knew, they were moving girls from Ireland to there, trafficking tricked and stolen east Europeans through their network, flying them over and over on the same routes between, most of the time, Belfast and Stockholm.

Ancuta was arrested by the PSNI and was to be extradited to Sweden. Once the Swedish were done with her, whether she was put in prison or not, the PSNI would be requesting to have her returned to Northern Ireland to answer their questions.

Two weeks later, in Bucharest, Ilie Ionut was tracked down and arrested as the ringleader of the whole thing. Again, he was to be extradited to Sweden and, after whatever happened there, he would be sent to Northern Ireland.

It was suddenly all moving in the right direction. There could be some justice.

The PSNI were clear that the information I had given to them about how and where they worked led to those pimps being brought down. But how much had they been brought down?

We would have to see. Trafficking is a difficult business. Most trafficked women will say very little to anyone about how they ended up in that position, and say even less about the people responsible for putting them there.

If you know about fear, control, psychology, then you know how this system works. If all you understand is that one person points at another person and says, 'They are the guilty one' and expect that is the job done, then you have no understanding at all.

Like a violated wife who never speaks, like an abused child who never tells, like a silent bullying victim, it is true that so many trafficked people – male and female – make the only choice they can, the wisest decision they can make in the circumstances, and that is to only say the things that will not put their health or the lives of loved ones at risk.

But for now I was extremely happy with the news of the arrests. I felt like I had kicked them, punched them back in the way that hurt them the most. They would have no shame, no concerns about loss of dignity or about their exposure as people of evil, but only that, very suddenly, they had been removed from doing what they most liked to do – control people and collect cash.

This felt like a new start for me, a point where the immediate danger of those who had most terrified me was gone.

Swedish police came to Northern Ireland to meet with the PSNI and, the plan was, to meet with me. Before that happened, the PSNI came to me again and discussed the Witness Protection option that they had brought up before.

I talked with their people and then with a lawyer who worked for the PSNI. Then I took my information home to Tom.

'They want me to think about this,' I said.

He shook his head. 'So do I,' he said. 'This is the safest possible move for you.'

'Yes,' I said, 'but for no one else.'

I would be a witness in court against them in Sweden and in Northern Ireland. In return I would be moved to another place, within the United Kingdom, and given a new identity. I would be set up with a home and a new start in life. I would not be able to contact anyone from my old life. Not my mother, not Tom.

'You're asking me,' he said, 'an impossible question.'

'That is what I wanted to hear,' I said. 'I don't want to leave you.'

We had become an item, formed a bond, joined together in a strange but strong way among our work to change things. It worked for us and we cared about each other's passion for progress. It seemed as if that would have to end. Had Ilie and Ancuta not taken enough from me?

I met again with the police and told them my feelings. I said I was very concerned about my mother, that she had been contacted so many times by these people, by people connected with them, and that I had no doubt that would happen again.

They told me it was a consideration I had to take on board. They said they could not provide the same option for my mother. I would, more or less, be leaving her at the mercy of people who had no mercy, who had made a life out of violence. What did that mean for her?

But, as the police said, I had so much to say in court, so much evidence and detail about the abuse I suffered, the injuries, about how they recruited and ditched girls, about how they worked us all day and night all over Ireland. I broke down as we spoke. It was one of the most difficult things I have ever been through.

And the Swedish police were waiting to talk, waiting to interview me about the couple they had in custody. I could not begin that conversation, the PSNI said, until I had agreed to be a witness.

Could I be an official witness in Operation Burgrave and not go into the protection programme?

'Yes,' they said, 'but you would have to end up hiding anyway, wouldn't you? The situation is the same and the same for your mother.'

Tom would not be leaving Belfast, running away with me and my mother with no money to some silly hideaway for the rest of our lives. Why would he? The idea was crazy. It was crazy for my mother too, for me to think that she might have any interest in doing that.

I said, 'No – I will not be a witness. I have helped you find these people, you must take it from here.'

The Swedish police went home after one week without ever speaking with me.

By now I was working at a golf club near Belfast, beginning to rebuild, now happier than I had been in a long time. I made arrangements to settle my tax bill and I was once again a legitimate person, earning some money, living at an address with a man that I liked so much.

It was a complicated time, a difficult time, because of what was going on with my pimps, but a positive one for me. It was the early days of the new start I spoke with you about, and my decision not to be disappeared into the wilderness made more sense as time went on.

I would move on and keep moving on.

I became more interested in my own health. I had one more tooth removed at the School of Dentistry in Belfast and was seeing a physiotherapist about my back and knees. My eyesight was getting worse, despite being used to having glasses again, and still my insomnia was driving me crazy. Insomnia, maybe, is the worst trouble of them all. Night after night, the loneliness of lying there and staring in the dark, muscles aching with exhaustion, brain whirling around, growing more and more angry with myself for not sleeping.

I was worried, deep down, about all of this. I could tell myself I was so happy that everything was moving along, but my crazy insomnia kept telling me my life was not normal. It was not in any way normal.

It might sound like I had a boyfriend, but, although Tom and I were close, I had problems, personal problems, which made us not completely a proper couple. And thinking about my own personal problems, about trying to deal with them, opened up more personal problems. I wanted to have none of this in my head, I wanted to mask it all, burn it all down, throw it all away in any way that I could. But night after night I was lying still and seeing things, hearing things, smelling things, fearing things.

I was a girl with secrets that could not be told, that were too awful to tell, so I did my best to pretend I had no secrets. And trying to be normal, to make friends and enjoy work and move along, was for me like trying to move through brick walls.

The question that came up again and again in my mind was, 'What am I doing? What on earth am I doing?'

The police told me Skinny would be giving evidence in Sweden. She had been arrested along with Ancuta in Belfast in April and deported to Sweden. Thirteen other girls had also been rescued, all linked to Ilie and Ancuta, but none was saying anything. At first Skinny had stuck to her story, that she only ever did webcam work, that she was a volunteer, that Ilie and Ancuta were not pimps. Yet eventually brave little Skinny had broken ranks and stood up for herself.

To the best of all that I know, she joined the Witness Protection Programme. She gave evidence against them in 2013 in Sweden, and what she was able to tell the people there, from the courtroom, shocked them.

Here is a piece from a newspaper:

Belfast Telegraph: 04/12/2013

Pair trafficking sex slaves out of Belfast are jailed in Sweden

By CHRIS KILPATRICK

GANG leaders who operated a prostitution network in Belfast and trafficked young women out of Northern Ireland have been jailed for four years.

Ilie Ionut (31) and his female associate, Ancuta Schwarz (28), were sentenced at a Swedish court yesterday for human trafficking, prostitution and aggravated procuring – the legal term for 'pimping'.

The convictions followed a huge police investigation involving the PSNI, Swedish and Romanian authorities.

Evidence presented to the court said Ionut controlled prostitution in Belfast and arranged for young women to be trafficked from Northern Ireland to other countries. Schwarz was accused of organising premises where the prostitution occurred.

*

The report went on to explain that some of the women involved were said to have been forced to have sex with up to 20 men a day and that the women were made to hand over most of the money they earned from selling sexual services. It also stated that the gang used threats, intimidation and physical violence to keep the women in line.

Furthermore, it said that 'Skinny' had been lured from her home to work posing for a web camera and promised a large income. But when she arrived in Ireland she was told there would be no web posing, only selling sex. It concluded that Prosecutors had said Ionut led the business, travelling from Northern Ireland to Sweden with several women over the past two years.

Four years was not enough. I don't know what I had been expecting, but maybe I thought it would be only good news once they got into court. Four years felt to me like a sentence a person should get for one single sex attack. A person who organises and tricks and fools and steals and arranges hundreds, thousands of sex attacks and rapes? Four years?

That was not what I had been expecting.

Chapter Twenty-Nine

One way to clear your head is to try to fill it with other things. In 2014, still working at the golf club, I signed up for a course of A levels.

I had researched and found that this was the best route into taking a degree in law. My busy mind kept coming back to the idea that the change in the law could be the best way forward, that it would change how this crime is seen, that it would help those who are victims of it. I hoped too that by making it much more clear that trafficking was such a hugely destructive thing, and such an increasing thing, a new law might lead to the courts being less lenient.

Ancuta and Ilie had been jailed of course in Sweden, but I had been told that, if they were to be jailed for similar crimes in Northern Ireland, the sentence would not be much different.

In September I began three A levels at Belfast Metropolitan College – English, History and Law. I had not completed my other degree in Romania, but I no longer wanted to. I felt I had more purpose to move ahead with what had become my new interest. A law degree from Queens University in Belfast, I was told, was a very good degree.

But cutting down my work hours to take the A level courses had left me too broke for comfort. I had to put them on hold. The little hopes of mine were, again, put on hold.

And things were not working out for me and Tom. He and I had been working with some journalists and I was getting more and more requests to discuss my story, and it was not good for my mind. Although we were a good team when it came to getting our voices heard, we decided to take a break from each other, from all the craziness we seemed to create.

I worked more, as much as I could, at the golf club, serving drinks and bringing food and laughing with the men and women who liked to talk about their sport.

It was normal that I would become friends with my manager, and normal that, knowing each other over time, he would want to know more about me. The police had called to speak with me one time and they had not been too discreet about that.

I reminded him that he had told me one time about a BBC Northern Ireland documentary about sex trafficking and he said he remembered that. I reminded him that he had spoken about the woman they had interviewed, the woman whose identity was hidden and who spoke of being kidnapped and sold and pimped out for sex across Ireland. And I told him that the woman was me.

His reaction could not have been more supportive, but I remember that I felt I should not have said what I had said. Even I was a fool with my own safety.

The truth is I just did not know how much of a risk I faced. Did Ilie and Ancuta know what I had said to the police? They must have known someone in Belfast had given information. And to my mind, there was a very good chance they would know that person was me.

Opening up my secret left me feeling stupid, as if I couldn't trust myself. I was in no danger from this person and this person would tell no one, but I had learned something about myself and I wasn't happy about it.

In February 2015, with all that on my mind, with the long daily walks to and from the golf club, with long hours of working and with sleep coming and going with no rhyme or reason, I quit my job there.

Tom and I had split and I was now living alone in a terraced house in south Belfast and again I had been asking myself what on earth I was doing.

I was still in touch with Tom and we still felt we had much to do, but we felt it was best for us to not be so close, at least not until I had dealt with some of what I needed to deal with.

I began a new job, carrying drinks and food once again, at a luxury hotel near Belfast. I needed to keep working to make money and I needed to be busy, I think, for the sake of my sanity.

When I started at the hotel, I didn't know much about it, that it was a place where the rich and famous would stay when they were in Belfast. I didn't recognise them, but Sean Bean and all the big *Game of Thrones* and *Lord of the Rings* people were there during the year I worked at the hotel. Dolly Parton too.

Towards the end of the year, after some time apart, I met with Tom once again. We updated each other on what we knew about any developments with the law, with getting it onto the law books. He told me that, in his conversations with MLAs and other political representatives, they had been referring to it as 'Anna's Law'.

I cannot tell you how much that lifted my heart.

I told him that, whatever happened, I was now set on following up on this plan to study law, to get a degree. It could be done, I said, if I saved enough for long enough and applied for the right loans.

Tom said he felt it was the right thing for me to consider, that he believed it was the right choice for me. He said that, whether the Anti-Trafficking Bill reached the law books or not, it was good that I wanted to continue down this road.

I told him I had been thinking of what I would tell them at the entrance interview, of how I would explain what I had been through.

I would say, 'Being a lawyer is not just about delivering sentiments from the law books, it is about protecting and helping human beings. It is a caring profession – or it should be a caring profession. It is not seen that way but I hope it can one day be seen that way. If it is working right, that's what it is. People who need help need the law. The law should be more than just a stop-off point; lawyers should be more than just bureaucrats.'

When I look at the Universal Declaration of Human Rights, I see how many of the rights so many people support are being denied to people every day. And I do not mean in brutal dictatorships. I mean in streets like yours, in houses like yours, in countries like yours, right now.

The UDHR is in one way like a list of things that people traffickers need to make sure you don't get in order for them to be successful with you, to make the most money from you.

It would be a wonderful thing, some day, to see that word – trafficking – written into that list in the way that 'slavery' is already there. I believe it is only a good thing, only in the interests of people all around the world, if we make that word bigger and clearer and see it in more places, to show that a trafficked person is nothing less than a person in slavery. The world is never going to fully see this hidden problem unless the problem is shown to it.

The new law would help trafficked women get education, support and safety. It would wipe out the defence that a trafficker can say the woman agreed to do it. These things are so important that to have had any influence on this happening, anywhere in the world, would have lifted my heart into the sky.

How much is trying worth?

But our journey was not going as smoothly as we had dared to hope. There was a problem with many members over one particular clause of the bill, Clause Six, which outlawed paying for sex.

In Northern Ireland it was illegal to kerb-crawl, pimp and run a brothel, but the act of buying a body for sex was not illegal. Clause Six would change all that. However, the Sinn Fein party were not convinced, and they were not alone. Some sex workers were also against this clause and were making plans to protest at Stormont. The police too did not have a great belief that it would be a good thing.

What mattered though was votes in Stormont and that was where we would fight if we had to. I was willing to meet with any MLAs who wanted to, to explain the human side of what they were talking about.

I know of course that there has always been sex for sale, but as I told you before there is now a terrible, growing form of sex for sale: it is modern-day sex slavery.

If you can tell a man, say a man in your town, that he might get arrested and end up in the papers because he has paid for sex, then he is less likely to do it. Not all men will stop, no. But fewer will do it.

And there is at least more hope that the women who are rescued from their slave work will not be treated like criminals, not be arrested, not be given criminal records and not just, as is sometimes the case in the UK, be deported back to their own countries, where the same criminal gang collects them and it all begins again.

And if there is a law against paying for sex in a certain country, the pimp will consider that before setting up business there.

The debate in Northern Ireland went over all of this again and again, inside and out, over and over.

On 21 October 2014, Northern Ireland voted in support of a big new law change. The assembly at Stormont voted 81 to 10 to bring in the bill launched by Lord Morrow. These would be the strongest anti-trafficking laws, whether the trafficking was for work or for sex, in the UK. And they included Clause Six – it would become illegal to buy sex in Northern Ireland.

The Justice Minister remained unsupportive, but in the end Sinn Fein came on board in what was seen as a very rare agreement between it and the DUP. There had been more than 60 amendments, but I could not have been happier to know that buying sex was now illegal.

On the same day, some sex workers wore masks and carried placards to protest the incoming bill. They said the law was 'disgraceful' and that Northern Ireland would be 'the laughing stock of Europe'.

I was there too on that day, and nothing anyone said could have brought me down. There were tears and hugs with all sorts of people, many of them people I had never met, who were as over the moon as I was.

It was a victory for all of us because so many people had played a part.

Lord Morrow gave me a copy of the bill, which I asked him to sign. And I asked everyone to sign. I keep it, like a treasure, in my home. It has the names of all sorts of people who were involved, supporters from all walks of life. I was asked to sign the bill that some others held too, and I remember thinking, as I looked at my own writing, that the letters had become so large, so happy, so rounded.

In January 2015, the bill officially became law.

Here is a BBC Northern Ireland website story from that day:

A bill that means Northern Ireland is the first part of the UK to make paying for sex a criminal offence has become effective after receiving Royal Assent …

The private members' bill was brought before the house by the Democratic Unionist Party (DUP) peer Lord Morrow …

'What has driven me throughout this entire process was the need to make a difference for the victims of this despicable trade,' he said.

'The testimonies of victims I have met will stay with me forever …'

Chapter Thirty

I met with Marco in January 2016, in Sibiu, Romania.

It had been hard to track him down, but contact was eventually made through a friend of Petre's and he was still in London. He was still there, still working, still smoking, still owing money, still moving along in his own way.

We must meet, I told him, in Sibiu as soon as possible.

And he agreed we would meet in January, that we would have a coffee together.

I am always uncomfortable in my home city, maybe I will always be uncomfortable in Romania, but this visit was for a good purpose. At the office where we got married, we got divorced. There was no argument, no complaints, no love lost. We officially separated and I got my own name back, my own self, my own life.

'Do you know my story?' I asked him afterwards.

'Yes,' he said, 'it is so terrible what happened to you, Anna.'

He said how he had tried to look after my property after I had gone, after my laptop, after people's keys, but he had been unable to keep track of everything.

I asked him, 'Do you know any people who take people, who traffic Romanian girls, Marco?'

'No,' he said, 'I have heard of it happening but I don't know anyone who does anything like that.'

'They pay money,' I said, 'because the right girl is worth so much money.'

'Yes,' he said.

'The girl can be used, over and over again, over and over, and keep her value for a long time,' I said. 'So much money can be made from a human being if they are treated like a product.'

'Yes,' he said.

'But a person would have to have a heart of evil to become involved in that,' I said.

'They would,' he said.

I do not think we will ever meet again.

I returned to Northern Ireland that month to news that Ilie Ionut and Ancuta Schwarz had been freed from jail in Sweden. But they did not get very far because, right away, they were extradited on two different flights to the UK, flown to Belfast from Stockholm. They appeared on separate dates at Belfast Magistrates Court to hear what they were facing.

Ancuta was charged with controlling prostitution and arranging sex trafficking, offences dating back to 2011. She walked into the dock that day wearing a long green coat with a leopard-print collar, like the coat of a pimp.

The court was told Ms Schwarz was alleged to have transferred £4,178 in criminal funds via money transfers to a woman in Romania and is alleged to have conspired to move other sums. She is also charged with aiding and abetting the control of prostitution and trafficking an individual in the UK for sexual exploitation.

That individual, I can tell you, is Skinny.

Ilie was told at first he faced four charges, including two counts of controlling prostitution for gain, human trafficking and removing criminal property from Northern Ireland. Their lawyers said they feared this was a case of 'double jeopardy' because they were in another courtroom in another jurisdiction but the charges were largely the same as those for which they had just served time.

And, of course, they were pleading not guilty to them all.

Or at least they did for four months. In May 2016, after a lot of behind-the-scenes talks, they pleaded guilty.

I can tell you that Ancuta smiled as the sentence was read out.

They would both serve just eight months inside for what they did while they were in Northern Ireland, and after that they would spend 16 months on supervised licence.

The police files said they were key members of 'an organised crime gang involved in controlling prostitution and human trafficking in Northern Ireland, Sweden and Romania'. They said how thirteen victims had been rescued as part of Operation Burgrave in Belfast. Victims, they said, were exploited with threats and violence, were isolated, had no money or documents and were dependent on the pimps.

Judge Kerr said there had been 'humiliating and degrading behaviour'.

'This is a case of organised crime which involved human trafficking – something which quite clearly is capable of causing potential physical and psychological injuries to victims at a high level,' he said, before giving them their short sentences.

But you know, I was not there, not at the hearing, not celebrating or weeping. I was not in Belfast, not in Northern Ireland, not anywhere near to where that part of my life had taken place. You see, as I had to do, I have moved on.

I have found someone, I have found a way forward, found work and study and a whole new life. Now I speak often with my old friend Mirela, and we laugh about the good times, make little plans for the future with the new friends we know.

And I am in contact with my mother, about good things, never bad things, about what I am doing, what I hope to do, who I hope to be.

I have connections in political circles, in the law, who have asked me to help with changing things, for advice on what the future should be for other countries.

I have met with senior figures in England and Scotland to discuss such matters, and I know I have much to contribute, much insight to bring, much value that cannot be measured in money.

Ancuta and Ilie know the inside of two jails because I was able to find them.

But as the months rolled on after my freedom was found, what became more important to me was that I was finding myself.

Perhaps this is the reason why, now, after all of this, I have chosen to return to university, to study law, to work in the future to try to change things.

One day, I know, my name will be struck from the record of criminals.

One day, I am certain, I will be told 'sorry' by important people, who will explain that they know as much as I know that I should never have seen the inside of the court in Galway.

They will know that what happened that day was an injustice, and the fact that I have been tagged as a criminal ever since is not the right telling of the story.

I am not what they said I am.

I am not a prostitute.

Testimonials

ONE:

Lord Maurice Morrow: Launched Private Members' Bill

Anna is a woman of immense fortitude. Her story broke my heart, absolutely stunned me. What is going on in this country, across the UK, in terms of human trafficking is horrifying. Anna proved to be an inspiration to me as I sought to bring the Human Trafficking and Exploitation Act through the Northern Ireland Assembly.

TWO:

Andy: Drug dealer

Anna was suicidal. That's what she was to me anyway. She didn't care about herself but she sort of just wanted to get a break from the life she had. That's what she was like when I met her. She was bruised all over. The people who did what they did to her, I wasn't involved, but they were given a hiding. They definitely were. They were given more than a hiding. It was what they deserved.

THREE:

Rachel Moran, author of *Paid For – My Journey Through Prostitution*

I first met Anna in 2014, while we were each engaged in supporting Lord Morrow's Human Trafficking and Exploitation

Bill, and I've since watched her weather every kind of storm, including the cruelty of strategically targeted lies that sought to deny the reality of her experience from those with a political interest in doing so. Despite everything, she never backed down, and we achieved our aim. I am glad of it – and enormously proud of her.

Acknowledgements

I want to thank those who helped during and after the months I spent under the control of others. They are many.

But I particularly thank the people referred to in this book as Tom and Andy. They believed in me when I had little left to believe in. They reached out when I was at my worst. They gave me hope.

Thanks also to fearless anti-prostitution campaigner Rachel Moran, to the extraordinarily caring people at Flourish NI, to Lord Maurice Morrow and to various charities and agencies that have done all they can. I truly know how precious kindness can be.

My thanks also to the Police Service of Northern Ireland for their assistance when writing this book, and more so for their relentless work to bring Ilie Ionut and Ancuta Schwarz to justice.

To my ghostwriter, Jason Johnson, a heart-felt thank you. You believed I could tell my story in full, if only once. You have been the sensitive, yet certain, driving force for this book.

To the most considerate and thoughtful literary agent, Paul Feldstein, and to my compassionate, understanding publishers, Ebury, I want to say that by taking on my story you have helped me to close a door and step away.

There are others too who have helped but who cannot be named. You know who you are.

I am unable to tell you who I am, where I am. The danger to myself and others, the police say, is too great.

But this story is bigger than one person, bigger than one place.

My dearest hopes are firstly that this book might bolster courage where it may be needed most.

And, secondly, that it will warn we are in a time of increasing, insidious slavery and that everyone, everywhere, should carefully consider what the next step is.

You can look and you can speak or, more comfortably, you can look away.

Anna.

Being a slave of fear is the worst type of slavery, George Bernard Shaw.

About the Authors

Jason Johnson is a journalist and writer from Northern Ireland.

Anna has worked behind the scenes with law-makers in Northern Ireland, playing an influential role in ushering in a radical new dawn of anti-sex trafficking laws. She no longer lives in the UK or Ireland.